1986

Past Masters
General Editor Keith Thomas

Spinoza

Roger Scruton is Professor of Philosophy and University Professor at Boston University. His books include *Kant*, also in the Past Masters series, *Sexual Desire*, and *Modern Philosophy*, along with several works of fiction.

Past Masters

Forthcoming

Roger Scruton

Spinoza

Oxford   New York

OXFORD UNIVERSITY PRESS

Oxford University Press, Walton Street, Oxford OX2 6DP

Oxford New York
Athens Auckland Bangkok Bombay
Calcutta Cape Town Dar es Salaam Delhi
Florence Hong Kong Istanbul Karachi
Kuala Lumpur Madras Madrid Melbourne
Mexico City Nairobi Paris Singapore
Taipei Tokyo Toronto

and associated companies in
Berlin Ibadan

Oxford is a trade mark of Oxford University Press

First published 1986 as an Oxford University Press paperback
Reissued 1996

British Library Cataloguing in Publication Data
Data available

Library of Congress Cataloging in Publication Data
Scruton, Roger.
Spinoza.
(Past Masters)
Bibliography: p.   Includes index.
1. Spinoza, Benedictus de, 1632–1677. 2. Philosophers
—Netherlands—Biography.   I. Title.   II. Series.
B3997.S34 1986   199'.492   86–12529
ISBN 0–19–287630–9 (pbk.)

10 9 8 7 6 5 4

Printed in Great Britain by
Biddles Ltd
Guildford and King's Lynn

Contents

Abbreviations

I have used the following abbreviations in referring to Spinoza's principal works:

C   *Correspondence*

E   *Ethics*

I   *Treatise on the Emendation of the Intellect (Tractatus de Intellectu Emendatione)*

M   *Metaphysical Thoughts* (Appendix to *Principles of Cartesian Philosophy*)

P   *Political Treatise (Tractatus Politicus)*

S   *Short Treatise on God, Man and his Well-being*

T   *Theologico-Political Treatise (Tractatus Theologico-Politicus)*

Where necessary I have used my own translations; otherwise, I have consulted the editions referred to at the end of this book, under Further Reading. A Glossary of Spinoza's principal terms, alerting the reader to variations in the standard translations of them, also occurs at the end of this work.

Preface

Spinoza's greatness and originality are hidden behind a remote, impassive, and often impenetrable style. Few have understood his arguments in their entirety; fewer still have recognized their continuing moral significance. I have presented no more than an outline, and am acutely aware of the injustice done, not only to Spinoza, but also to the patient scholars who have wrestled with his meaning. My primary object has been to describe, in simple language, the contours of a complex system of thought. Even so, I have been unable to make Spinoza's theory of substance fully accessible, and Chapter 3 must therefore be read twice if it is to be understood.

I have benefited from many students and friends, and in particular from David Murray, whose erudition saved me from several errors of interpretation. I have also benefited from Joanna North, whose unpublished work suggested ways of translating Spinoza's most awkward conceptions into terms that are intelligible and interesting to the modern reader. I am grateful to her, not only for the chance to read and discuss her work, but also for her detailed criticisms of my own. She has no part in the failings of this book, but a considerable part in its virtues, if it has any.

London, September 1985

1 Life and character

Benedict (Baruch) de Spinoza (1632–77) lived in the Netherlands at a time when scientific discovery, religious division, and profound political change had revolutionized the nature and application of philosophy. While he joined eagerly in the contemporary intellectual battles, philosophy was, for Spinoza, not a weapon but a way of life, a sacred order whose servants were transported to a supreme and certain blessedness. But every order requires a sacrifice, and that demanded by philosophy—the adoption of truth as one's master and one's goal—is neither easily undertaken, nor readily understood by those who refuse it. To the mass of mankind, therefore, the philosopher may appear as a spiritual saboteur, a subverter of things lawfully established, and an apologist for the devil. So Spinoza appeared to his contemporaries, and for many years after his death he was regarded as the greatest heretic of the seventeenth century.

Spinoza's ancestors were Spanish Jews, who had settled during the sixteenth century on the borders of Spain and Portugal, there to maintain a flourishing trade. For several centuries such people had lived relatively securely in the Spanish peninsula, protected by the Muslim princes, and mingling openly with their Islamic neighbours. Their theologians and scholars had joined in the great revival of Aristotelian philosophy, and one of them—Moses ben Maimon (Maimonides, 1135–1204)—had exerted a far-reaching influence, not only over Judaism, but also over Islam and Christianity. It was Maimonides, indeed, who did most to set medieval theology upon its Aristotelian path—a path which led, at last, to the strange stark theism, which many denounced as atheism, of Spinoza.

When the kingdom of Granada was conquered by Ferdinand and Isabella, and the Arabs were finally expelled from the peninsula, an epoch of vengeance began. Christ's enemies were now assiduously punished for crimes of which they had been hitherto unaware. To save themselves from the Inquisition Jews were obliged either to convert or to emigrate, and the multitude of converted Jews—vulgarly known as *marranos*—led a miserable existence, under the vigilant eye of an Inquisition that could never quite believe in the sincerity of a conversion induced by itself. (The term *marrano* is sometimes thought to derive from the obscure sentence in 1 Corinthians 16: 22: 'If any man loveth not the Lord, let him be *anathema maranatha*'. It could also be a corruption of *morisco*—'moor'. However, its everyday meaning in Spanish is 'pig'.)

The Spanish monarchy's intolerable combination of spiritual tyranny and secular arrogance provoked at last the revolt which initiated its decline. From the desperate rising of a handful of subjects in the Netherlands there sprang a new commonwealth, and one which promised to be as free and tolerant as the Arabian princedoms of Spain. In the spring of 1593 a small body of *marranos* sailed secretly from Portugal, attracted by the decree of toleration which had been made in 1579 by the Union of Utrecht, when the seven northern provinces, combining against their Spanish sovereign, had sought the protection of the great William I of Orange (William the Silent). Calling at Emden the *marranos* were advised by the German Jews of East Friesland to make for Amsterdam, where they promptly reverted to the ancestral faith which the Inquisition, despite the most ingenious methods, had failed to eradicate.

The causes of the revolt in the Netherlands were many,

but principal among them was the advance made by the Reformation, and the desire to establish sufficient freedom of worship to permit the Reformed churches to exist, and their congregations to live and prosper. The war with Spain continued spasmodically until the peace of Munster in 1648, and during this time the strange new commonwealth defined its borders and began to prosper within them. Known retrospectively as the Dutch Republic, it was in reality a loose association of medieval cities, represented by an 'Estates General' whose answerability was never precisely or legally defined. Nominally above the Estates General, but also appointed by them, stood the Stadtholder. Partly from gratitude, partly for the sake of convenience and continuity, this office was conferred on the House of Orange. The Southern Provinces had stayed loyal to the Spanish crown, and retained the Roman Catholic religion; during the years following the assassination of William, therefore, when his descendants exercised successively the powers of the Stadtholder, the Spanish threat to the Northern Provinces was popularly conceived in religious terms. Catholicism became the enemy, and whatever religious toleration had been intended by William, it soon became clear that it would not be extended to the Catholics, who found themselves in a position comparable to that of the *marranos* in Spain.

Furthermore, as the Calvinist Church manoeuvred itself into supreme religious authority in the North, it brought its own peculiar sense of spiritual danger. The doctrine of predestination rapidly became orthodoxy, and—as with every belief upon which a social and political system is founded—it had to be protected from the assaults of unbelievers. The followers of Arminius, professor of theology at Leyden, refused to accept those propositions of the Calvinist doctrine which seemed to fly in the face of reason, and issued in 1610 a 'Remonstrance', setting forth their dissident opinions, and requesting the Estates General to uphold the freedom of worship and opinion which had been guaranteed at Utrecht. The Stadtholder, Prince Maurice of Orange, declared against the Remonstrants, and those who spoke out in favour of religious freedom began to feel the pinch of established power. In the ensuing conflict, the greatest Dutch thinker of the time—the jurist Hugo Grotius—was sentenced at Maurice's instigation to life imprisonment, from which he subsequently escaped into exile. And in 1619 the Synod of Dort defined the Dutch Church as a 'community of the elect', thereby establishing orthodox Calvinism as the official religion of the Republic, and authorizing the purging of universities and other places of influence.

Nevertheless, the new Church was unable to suppress the thoughts which disturbed it. Partly on account of the loose structure of the Republic—in which the undefined powers of Estates General and Stadtholder could not be combined into a single-minded tyranny—and partly on account of the legacy of Utrecht, with its declared ideal of a purely secular government, the spirit of toleration continued to breathe, and those Remonstrants who were content to establish themselves apart were allowed to live in relative tranquillity. At the same time, there flourished around them an equally remarkable, and for us more interesting, defiance of the Calvinist spirit: the art and culture of the Netherlands, in which man's relation to the world of objects, and to his own physical life, became the subject of a profound spiritual interrogation.

Into this extraordinary new order came the *marranos*, welcomed at first as fellow victims of Spanish cruelty. Permission to build a synagogue was granted in 1598, and in 1615 the Estates General passed a regular ordinance for the admission and government of the Jews. Thereafter the Jewish community began to prosper, being regarded as less threatening to the orthodox religion than the dissenting sects which called themselves Christian, and yet which admitted (what was acknowledged on both sides to be true) that they were not elected to salvation.

As is natural in exile communities, the Jews of Amsterdam were jealous of their identity, maintaining a severe edict of vigilance against those who would pervert a faith proved by so much suffering. New arrivals were expected to make fervent demonstrations of their orthodoxy. It was not sufficient for the *marranos* to cast off the habits of an enforced Christianity. It was necessary also that they be freshly instructed in the Mosaic law and the Jewish observances, by the Ashkenazi rabbis of Amsterdam, who were deeply suspicious of the Sephardic traditions of Spain. The rabbinical fear of heresy thereby came to mirror the fear expressed by the Calvinist Church towards those who questioned its feebler doctrines; it was further exacerbated by the Popish habit and demeanour of the newcomers, and by the occasional scandalous eruption of unbelief. The Jewish community was particularly shaken by the antics of one Uriel da Costa who, prompted more by mental instability than by principle, rebelled against the formalistic teaching of the synagogue, was twice excommunicated, and twice reconciled after a humiliating penance, and who finally shot himself, disgusted with a world that had permitted so much indecision in a creature born for higher things. The memory of this scandal contributed to the religious panic as a result of which the community was to expel, as unworthy of its protection, the greatest genius who had grown within its care.

Spinoza's father Michael had probably come to

Amsterdam as a child, before the full establishment and recognition of the Jewish colony. As a successful merchant, with good connections, he rose rapidly to a position of influence, becoming Warden of the synagogue and of the Amsterdam Jewish school. His life was marred, however, by private sorrow: he buried three wives, and of his six children, only two—Baruch and his half-sister Rebekah—survived into adulthood.

Baruch de Spinoza was born on 24 November 1632, and attended, as a child, the Jewish school and the synagogue, where he studied Hebrew and the works of Jewish and Arabian theologians. Among his early teachers were the orthodox senior rabbi of Amsterdam, Rabbi Saul Morteira, and the liberal Rabbi Manasseh ben Israel, a man of wide learning and secular interests, friend of Vossius, Grotius, and Rembrandt, who was to take a leading part in promoting the re-admission of the Jews to England. (Manasseh thereby became the target of a polemic from the Puritan Prynne who, despite his heartfelt disgust towards both tyrants and Jews, failed to see why the Jews are accused of murdering Christian children only when tyrants need money.) It was no doubt through Manasseh's influence that Spinoza began to identify so strongly with the secular and enquiring culture of the Netherlands.

Spinoza's father hoped that he might become a rabbi, and therefore made available to him as many educational opportunities as seemed compatible with orthodoxy. At the age of twenty, Spinoza began to take lessons from the teacher Frances Van den Enden, who introduced him to the scholastic philosophy that was to provide so much of the terminology of Spinoza's *Ethics*. Van den Enden also filled him with enthusiasm for modern science, and no doubt spoke to him of the new philosophy of Descartes. Contact with secular and Christian ways of thinking increased

Spinoza's dissatisfaction with the biblical interpretations he received from the rabbis, who in turn frowned on his interest in natural science, and on his study of the pernicious Latin language, in which so much heresy and blasphemy had been so engagingly expressed.

Spinoza's growing independence of mind led him to sympathize with the unorthodox Christians of the Netherlands, and in particular with the Collegiants (an anti-clerical sect of Remonstrants) and the Mennonites, who had come into being a century earlier, but who identified closely with the Remonstrant movement. Their simple life-style and tolerant practice provided a moral archetype that Spinoza was to defend in his writings. His association with these sects did Spinoza no good in the eyes of the synagogue, and matters were exacerbated when his sister Rebekah tried to block Spinoza's share of the inheritance due on his father's death in 1654. Spinoza, we are told, took his sister to court, established his claim, and then calmly renounced it, along with his remaining loyalty to a community whose values he did not share. He adopted the name Benedict, went to live with Van den Enden, and began to teach in his school, becoming more and more immersed in the intellectual concerns of the secular and Christian thinkers with whom he now associated.

Van den Enden's school was already notorious in Amsterdam as a centre of free enquiry, and by 1656 Spinoza's life was so great a scandal to the Jewish community, that it could no longer be endured. J. M. Lucas, a friend of Spinoza's who wrote his biography, tells us that two young acquaintances from the synagogue came at this time to interrogate the philosopher concerning his religious opinions. He is said to have maintained, not only that God has a body, but that nothing in the scriptures could be adduced that would tend to the contrary opinion. The two men left in anger, and, according to another story, embellished by Bayle, Spinoza was subsequently attacked on the steps of the synagogue. He is said to have kept by him thereafter the cloak which had been torn by his assailant's dagger.

The Jewish community was under considerable strain, due partly to a sudden and unpopular influx of Polish Jews, who had escaped from the Muscovite and Cossack invasions of Poland. Nevertheless, it could fairly be said that the rabbis over-reacted to Spinoza's eccentric life-style, and that the cause of Judaism might have been better served by ignoring someone who had no natural disposition to draw attention to his dissent from it. Wisely or not, however, the rabbis summoned Spinoza before them, accused him of heresy, and urged him in vain to repent. After a thirty-day period of excommunication Spinoza was judged to be incorrigible; on 27 July 1656 he was finally cast out of the synagogue, and was anathematized 'with the anathema wherewith Joshua anathematized Jericho', to wit:

cursed be he by day, and cursed be he by night; cursed be he when he lieth down, and cursed be he when he riseth up; cursed be he when he goeth out and cursed be he when he cometh in; the Lord will not pardon him; the wrath and fury of the Lord will be kindled against this man, and bring down upon him all the curses which are written in the Book of the Law; and the Lord will destroy his name from under the heavens; and, to his undoing, the Lord will cut him off from all the tribes of Israel, with all the curses of the firmament which are written in the Book of the Law; but ye that cleave unto the Lord God live all of you this day!

We ordain that no one may communicate with him

verbally or in writing, nor show him any favour, nor stay under the same roof with him, nor be within four cubits of him, nor read anything composed or written by him.

To which Spinoza is said to have replied: 'Very well; this does not force me to do anything that I would not have done of my own accord, had I not been afraid of a scandal.' Spinoza did not rejoice in this conflict, however. On the contrary, after his excommunication he addressed to the elders of the synagogue an *Apology* (written in Spanish), in which he defended his views as orthodox, and condemned the rabbis for accusing him of 'horrible practices and other enormities' merely because he had neglected ceremonial observances. Unfortunately no copies of this apology survive, though its contents were probably later included in the *Theologico-Political Treatise*.

The civil authorities, responding to the appeals of the rabbis, and also of the Calvinist clergy, who had been vicariously offended by the existence of a free-thinker in the synagogue, banished Spinoza for a time from Amsterdam. After a short spell in the village of Ouwerkerk, he returned to the city, and until 1660 supported himself by giving private lessons in Cartesian philosophy and by grinding lenses. During this period Spinoza composed the *Short Treatise on God, Man and his Well-being*, of which two Dutch translations survive, discovered about 1810. This book contains the main elements of Spinoza's later philosophy, albeit rather crudely expressed.

In 1660 Spinoza went to the quiet country village of Rijnsburg, near Leyden, where the Collegiants had established their headquarters. His reputation as a learned man had spread, and he began to receive visits and correspondence from enquiring people anxious to discuss with him the philosophical and scientific questions that were stirring the mind and heart of Europe. One of these was Henry Oldenburg (?1615–77), a learned theologian and diplomat, who was to become the first secretary of the newly-formed Royal Society in London, and whose correspondence with Spinoza is one of the most valuable sources for the student of Spinoza's philosophy. At Rijnsburg Spinoza composed, in Latin, the first part of an exposition of Descartes' metaphysics, entitled *Principles of Cartesian Philosophy*, and began work on his masterpiece, the *Ethics* (also written in Latin). In 1663 he left Rijnsburg for Voorburg, passing through Amsterdam, where his friends persuaded him to complete the exposition of Descartes, and to publish it, together with an appendix of his own 'metaphysical thoughts'. Spinoza completed the task in two weeks, such rapidity testifying not to the author's haste, but to his absolute familiarity with the system whose main ideas he sought to expound. Spinoza's friend Lodewijk Meyer (1630–81) added a preface in which, at the author's request, he informed the reader that Spinoza did not agree with all the Cartesian arguments. The book was the only one to be published by Spinoza under his own name: it is now unjustly neglected, although at the time it enjoyed a high repute among the learned, most of whom were students of the Cartesian system, and many of whom were taken aback to see the system geometrically expounded, and its defects laid bare.

At Voorburg Spinoza continued to work on the *Ethics* and to correspond with scientists, philosophers and theologians. He became acquainted with Christian Huygens, the founder of modern optics, with Johan Hudde, Burgomaster of Amsterdam, and, probably through Hudde, with Jan de Witt, the enlightened statesman who held the office of Grand Pensionary of the Netherlands. According to many analysts, more executive power was vested in the

Grand Pensionary than was exercised either by the Stadtholder or by the Estates General. Jan de Witt was an energetic defender of those principles of tolerance and free speech upon which the Dutch Republic had been founded, and also, through the command over foreign relations bestowed upon him by his office, a subtle and effective advocate of the Netherlands' interests.

In 1652–4 the Netherlands had been at war with England, partly as a result of tensions generated by the Act of Navigation, whereby Dutch shipping was harassed and blockaded, and the trade and fishing upon which the Republic depended for its livelihood seriously impaired. Jan de Witt had mediated in this quarrel. He had succeeded, however, only in gaining the acceptance of the Estates to Cromwell's demand that the young Prince of Orange (grandson of William I) should not lead the military forces of the Netherlands. This settlement exacerbated the generic conflict between the Stadtholder and the Estates, and Jan de Witt—already regarded by the Stadtholder as too frank an advocate of religious liberty—was henceforth suspected by the Orangist party.

As so often in the Netherlands, the growing political tension found expression in controversies over the nature of the state, and the desirability or otherwise of free worship and free opinion. Spinoza's friendship with de Witt caused him to take sides in the dispute, and the resulting *Theologico-Political Treatise*, published anonymously in 1670, contained a powerful defence of secular and constitutional government. In the words of Sir Frederick Pollock, 'the tone and form of the treatise are conciliatory, but with the kind of high-handed conciliation that exasperates'. The identity of the author did not remain for long concealed, and this work, which advocated tolerance, understanding and the ways of peace, drew down upon

Spinoza the belligerent apostrophes of all those who stood (as they thought) to lose from such dangerous policies. De Witt's enemies described the *Treatise* as 'forged in Hell by a renegade Jew and the Devil, and issued with the knowledge of Jan de Witt'. The work was condemned by the Synod of the Reformed Church in 1673, and formally banned in 1674.

In 1670 Spinoza moved to the Hague, where he lived upon a small allowance of 500 florins (£40) a year, composed of a small pension granted annually by Jan de Witt, and an annuity from the brother of his dead friend, Simon de Vries. (De Vries had wished to make Spinoza his heir, but had been dissuaded from this course by Spinoza's honourable pleading on behalf of De Vries's family.) For the next five years he continued to work on his *Ethics*, wrote an unfinished grammar of the Hebrew language, and began the *Political Treatise*. He also wrote two scientific essays—'On the Rainbow', and 'On the Calculation of Chances'—and began a Dutch translation (the unfinished fragments of which he destroyed) of the Bible. His modest income and dedication kept him confined to his lodgings, where he would sometimes remain without venturing forth for three months at a time.

In 1665 the Netherlands had again been at war with England, and Jan de Witt had managed to stop the bloodshed by forging, in 1668, the triple alliance between the Netherlands, England and Sweden. In 1671, however, Charles II of England joined forces against the Dutch with Louis XIV of France; war was declared in 1672, and 120,000 French troops marched into the Netherlands. The populace, in a state of panic, and well schooled in faction, blamed the disaster on de Witt, and looked—as always in a time of crisis—to the House of Orange as their natural source of leadership. The Orangists did nothing to quell the rumours of the Grand Pensionary's treachery, and on 20 August 1672 de Witt and his brother were seized at the Hague and brutally beaten to death by a furious crowd.

It is said that Spinoza, on hearing of this outrage, prepared to sally forth to the scene of the crime, with a notice marked *Ultimi Barbari*. It is just possible that the populace would have understood such an inscription; in any case, Spinoza's uncharacteristic outburst was overcome by Van der Spyck, the painter in whose house he resided. Later Spinoza was to become the object of the same mindless fury that had cost the life of his patron. In 1677 he undertook a mission of peace to the French army based at Utrecht, having been invited, on behalf of the great Condé, by Colonel Stoupe. Spinoza's mission seems to have had the sanction of the Dutch authorities. Nevertheless, returning from Utrecht, after weeks of pointless waiting, Spinoza was greeted with intense suspicion. To the charges of heretic and atheist was now added that of spy, and his landlord feared that his house might be besieged by the infuriated mob. Spinoza comforted him with these words:

> Fear nothing on my account; I can easily justify myself; there are people enough, and of the chief men in the country too, who well know the motives of my journey. But whatever comes of it, so soon as the crowd makes the least noise at your door, I will go out and make straight for them, though they should serve me as they have done the unhappy de Witts. I am a good republican, and have never had any aim but the honour and welfare of the state.

While with the French forces Spinoza was asked to dedicate a book to Louis XIV, in return for a royal pension. He politely refused. In the same year came another, and more honourable, offer: this time of a professorship at the

University of Heidelberg. The invitation came from the Elector Palatine, Prince Karl Ludwig, and was transmitted to Spinoza in the following terms: 'You will have the most ample freedom in philosophical teaching, which the prince is confident you will not misuse, to disturb the religion publicly established'. In answer, Spinoza remarked that such a clause, imposing undefined limits on his intellectual freedom, was not one with which he could comply. 'Religious quarrels,' he added, 'do not arise so much from ardent zeal for religion, as from men's various dispositions and love of contradiction, which causes them habitually to distort and condemn everything, however rightly it may have been said. I have experienced these effects in my private and secluded station; how much more should I have to fear them after my elevation to this post of honour' (*C* XLVIII). Spinoza therefore declined the offer, and remained in frugal retirement at the Hague.

From there he continued to correspond with his distinguished contemporaries, including the young scientist von Tschirnhaus, a Bohemian count who travelled widely in pursuit of instruction. Tschirnhaus's letters contain the most important of the objections that were offered to Spinoza's *Ethics*, a book which was then circulating in manuscript, and drawing lively interest from the learned world. Through Tschirnhaus Spinoza made the acquaintance of Leibniz, who was already familiar with some of his writings. The letters between the two philosophers were cordial, although Spinoza at first distrusted Leibniz, who in turn referred to him privately as 'a Jew expelled from the synagogue for his monstrous opinions'. Since the fundamental assumptions behind their two systems are profoundly similar, it is perhaps not surprising that the two philosophers—whose conclusions are wholly opposed— should have treated each other with a certain caution.

Several of Spinoza's friends hoped that he would publish the *Ethics*. In a letter to Oldenburg, Spinoza explained his reasons for withholding the book from the press:

> . . . I had set out to Amsterdam for the purpose of publishing the book I had mentioned to you. While I was negotiating, a rumour gained currency that I had in the press a book concerning God, wherein I endeavoured to show that there is no God. Hence certain theologians, perhaps the authors of the rumour, took occasion to complain of me before the prince and magistrates; moreover, the stupid Cartesians, being suspected of favouring me, endeavoured to remove the aspersions by abusing everywhere my opinions and writings, a course which they still pursue. When I became aware of this through trustworthy men, who also assured me that the theologians were everywhere lying in wait for me, I determined to put off publishing till I saw how things were going . . . (*C* LXVIII)

In the event things got worse, and Spinoza gave up the idea of publishing the *Ethics*, believing that it would create such a cloud of hostility as to obscure, in the minds even of reasonable people, the real meaning of its arguments. Meanwhile, the book was read attentively, and at least one club existed for the express purpose of working through its proofs.

Spinoza's health began to fail in 1676. For some time he had been suffering from consumption, a condition that had doubtless been exacerbated by his work as a lens-grinder. He remained active, however, and uncomplaining. Only at the end did he signal to the world his imminent departure from it. On Saturday, 20 February 1677 Spinoza sent for his friend and physician, Dr G. H. Schuller. He spent the afternoon, as was his custom, with his host's family, and then went early to bed. Schuller arrived on the Sunday to find the philosopher in better spirits; the Van der Spycks left him in the afternoon to attend the Lutheran church, and learned on their return that Spinoza had died at three o'clock. He was buried in the cemetery of the New Church on the Spuy, apparently in a hired grave. It is said that six coaches attended the funeral, and that many prominent citizens came to pay their last respects. The headstone marking Spinoza's grave still stands, although the grave itself was probably hired again, and the philosopher's bones removed from it.

Shortly after Spinoza's death his friend Colerus, subsequently Lutheran pastor at the Hague, composed a biographical memoir. From this we learn of the simplicity and naturalness of Spinoza's life and character, and of the high esteem in which he was held by his acquaintances and friends. The seclusion of Spinoza's life was necessitated by intense labour and intellectual discipline, and his frugality expressed independence of spirit rather than meanness or self-concern. The strength of Spinoza's social feelings, and his Aristotelian emphasis on friendship as a necessary human good, are abundantly shown in the *Ethics*. His two biographers—Colerus and J. M. Lucas, both of whom had know him intimately and loved him well—testify to his personal charm, nobility of outlook, and affectionate disposition. Their testimony is confirmed by Spinoza's own words, in a letter:

> So far as in me lies, I value, above all other things out of my control, the joining hands of friendship with men who are lovers of truth. I believe that nothing in the world, of things outside our own control, brings more peace than the possibility of affectionate intercourse with such men; it is just as impossible that the love we

16

bear them can be disturbed (inasmuch as it is founded on the desire each feels for the knowledge of truth), as that truth once perceived should not be assented to.

(*C* XIX)

In that utterance is contained, however, a highly metaphysical view of friendship, and one to which we shall have cause to return.

Lucas tells us that Spinoza was of medium height and genial expression. Several portraits exist, although their authenticity is not established. Spinoza was himself interested in the prevailing pastime of the Netherlands, and would pass many hours sketching with ink and paper. He smoked a pipe, and drank beer—as is shown by his gratitude, expressed in a letter, for a gift of half a tun (*C* LXXII). In dress he was conventional and tidy, holding that 'an affectation of negligence is the mark of an inferior mind, in which wisdom is not to be found at all, and in which the sciences can only breed impurity and corruption'.

Of Spinoza's attitude to the other sex little is known, although it has been claimed that Spinoza was captivated, as a young man of twenty-three, by Van den Enden's daughter, Clara Maria, who rejected him in favour of a richer pupil. Some discredit this story, on the grounds that the girl was probably not more than twelve years old at the time. On the other hand, Spinoza is the only great philosopher to have written with insight on the subject of sexual jealousy (*E* 3, 35), and his remarks suggest a deep familiarity with the emotion described. Lucas tells us that, while Spinoza did not condemn marriage, he rejected it for himself, perhaps fearing the 'ill temper of a woman', and in any case recognizing in matrimony a threat to his scholarly interests.

Spinoza's *Ethics* is a work of concentrated argument and

immense intellectual ambition. It is therefore not surprising that Spinoza wrote little else, besides the works already mentioned. An early *Treatise on the Emendation of the Intellect* was left unfinished, as was the *Political Treatise*, upon which Spinoza was working when he died. After his death, his loyal friends Jelles, Meyer and Schuller gathered together the philosopher's correspondence, and published those parts which seemed to be of scientific interest, together with the *Ethics*, and the first of the unfinished treatises. The editors did not dare to add their names to the publication, which was quickly sold out, and as quickly banned. The style of these works is sparse, unadorned, and yet solemn and imposing; the occasional aphorisms jump from the page with all the greater force, in that they appear as the surprising but necessary consequences of arguments presented with mathematical exactitude.

Spinoza's mother-tongue was Spanish; he was a master of Hebrew and had an effective command of Portuguese and Dutch—perhaps also of French. However, none of those languages contained the wealth of scientific and philosophical argument that was contained in Latin, which language therefore became, for Spinoza, both the primary vehicle of his thought, and the symbol of his intellectual quest. In choosing the universal language of our culture, Spinoza wrote the last indisputable Latin masterpiece, and one in which the refined conceptions of medieval philosophy are finally turned against themselves and destroyed entirely. He chose a single word from that language for his device: *caute*—'be cautious'—inscribed beneath a rose, the symbol of secrecy. For, having chosen to write in a language that was so widely intelligible, he was compelled to hide what he had written.

2 Background

Spinoza left a celebrated description of his life's endeavour:

> After experience had taught me that all things which frequently take place in ordinary life are vain and futile; when I saw that all the things I feared and which feared me had nothing good or bad in them save in so far as the mind was affected by them, I determined at last to inquire whether there might be anything which might be truly good and able to communicate its goodness, and by which the mind might be affected to the exclusion of all other things: I determined, I say, to inquire whether I might discover and acquire the faculty of enjoying throughout eternity continual supreme happiness.
>
> (*I* i)

It was the affectation of the age to present its conceptions in this way—each as a wholly new departure, a working out *ab initio* of an answer unpolluted by received ideas and free from customary falsehoods. But it is perhaps truer of Spinoza than of his contemporaries, that his enterprise was one of radical deduction from first principles. Even he, however, did not think in a historical vacuum, or without reference—however covert—to conceptions whose meaning has clouded with time, and whose plausibility is no longer obvious.

Spinoza began to learn Latin when he was twenty. Until then, he had access to seventeenth-century thought and literature only through discussion with his companions and teachers, and through the occasional Spanish or

Hebrew translation. We must inevitably conclude, therefore, that the main influences over Spinoza's thought during his formative years were not those philosophers, such as Descartes, to whom he later devoted his attention, but the Jewish and Muslim writers of earlier centuries, whose thoughts provided the main arguments of contemporary Judaism. Through the works of Moses Maimonides and the commentaries of the Arab Averroës, Spinoza would have become acquainted with Aristotle. These and later theologians would also have introduced him to the ideas of the Christian scholastics. In Maimonides he would have encountered the image of philosophy as a guide to life; in the Kabbalah the conceptions of God's immanence, and of the ultimate identity between the Creator and his creation. In the Talmud, and again in Maimonides, he would have seen an obsessive love of moral detail—a minute examination of human passion and action, combined with a suspicion of the schematic morality of abstract principle. All those ideas resurge in the *Ethics*, in remarkable and transmuted form. But by the time Spinoza came to write that work, two further influences had changed his conception, both of the questions of philosophy, and of the method which could answer them. These two influences were Descartes, from whom Spinoza took his conception of metaphysics as the foundation of scientific knowledge; and the new works of political philosophy—in particular those of Grotius and Hobbes—which attempted to set man within the whole context of his social nature and political circumstance, and to derive the precepts best suited to his finite and erroneous condition.

Of all those influences, it is difficult now to single out any one as decisive. Modern scholarship has made it impossible to accept the traditional interpretation of Spinoza, as the most systematic of Descartes' disciples, the metaphysical purist who sought to reconcile the contradictions, and rectify the science, of his master. It is as easy to see Spinoza as one of the last great representatives of medieval thinking, who attempted to reconcile an Aristotelian theology with the findings of modern science, and to provide for the new man of the Enlightenment a theory of human nature, and of human happiness, that would vindicate the life of contemplation which for Aristotle was the highest good for man.

Spinoza would have condemned the practice (known nowadays as the 'history of ideas') whereby a study of the ancestry of ideas takes precedence over an enquiry into their truth and meaning. Philosophy, he remarked, should be judged apart from the life and studies of its exponents (*T* vii). Nevertheless, his own ideas and arguments will seem so strange at first sight to the modern reader, as to be scarcely intelligible without reference to their antecedents. As I shall later try to show, it was by no means a fault in Spinoza that he paid so much attention to ideas which had passed their prime. On the contrary, it was the total vision of Aristotelian and scholastic philosophy which helped to frame Spinoza's theory of the universe: a theory that showed exactly how we could know the world, act on it, and find our happiness within it. Spinoza's achievement was to show man and his world as an inextricable unity, and man himself as simultaneously master and servant of the fate which creates him.

Aristotelian and scholastic metaphysics
It is impossible to understand either Spinoza or Descartes without referring to a concept inherited through the scholastics from Aristotle: the concept of substance. According to Aristotelian logic, every simple proposition contains two parts—subject and predicate—reflecting a fundamental division in reality, between substances, and

the attributes which are 'predicated of', 'attributed to', or which 'inhere in' them. (In the proposition 'John is bald', for example, baldness is predicated of John.) This logical distinction has metaphysical implications. Since substances can change in respect of their attributes, they must endure through change. Indeed, there is a temptation contained in the very idea of substance—a temptation majestically yielded to by Spinoza—to suppose that substances endure through every change, and can therefore be neither created nor destroyed. Moreover, if we can refer to substances it must be possible to separate them, at least in thought, from the attributes with which they might at some particular moment be encumbered. Hence we should distinguish the 'essence' of substance—that without which it could not be the particular thing that it is—from its 'accidents': the properties in respect of which it might change without ceasing altogether to be. Finally no attribute can exist without a substance in which it inheres: attributes are essentially dependent. It is therefore substances, according to the Aristotelian vision, which are the ultimate constituents of reality.

Aristotelian science consisted in the classification of substances into genera and species. The new science of Bacon and Galileo took quantity and not quality as the decisive factor in the explanation of change, and therefore fretted against the bonds imposed upon it by the restricting concept of substance. In particular, it was hampered by the insensitivity of this concept to the distinction between individual and species terms on the one hand, and quantitative (or 'mass') terms on the other. For example, 'man'—which can denote both an individual and the class which subsumes him—refers to individual substances. It also expresses a predicate which generally describes them. But what about 'snow' and 'water'? There are not individual 'snows' or 'waters', except in an attenuated sense which would seem to obliterate a distinction fundamental to scientific thought. This is the distinction between 'thing' and 'stuff', between what can be counted, and what can only be measured. The difficulty of forcing the idea of 'stuff' into the conceptual frame of 'substance' is responsible for much of the rejection during the seventeenth century of Aristotelian science, and for this reason, if for no other, the concept of substance was bound to occupy the central role which Spinoza accorded to it in his philosophy.

Medieval theology inherited other arguments and conceptions from Aristotle and the post-Aristotelian corpus, and many of its original contributions are marked by the unmistakable tone of Aristotelian metaphysics. This is especially true of what was to be the most influential of all scholastic arguments: the ontological proof of God's existence. The discovery of this proof is normally credited to St Anselm, Archbishop of Canterbury (1033–1109), but it is not too great a distortion to find glimpses of it in certain passages of Aristotle's *Metaphysics*, and in the commentaries on that work written by Al-Farabi and Ibn Sinna (Avicenna). It was rejected by St Thomas Aquinas in his systematic exposition of the basis of Christian doctrine, but nevertheless belongs to a class of arguments others of which he was inclined to accept, and all of which derive their proof for the existence of God by way of the concept of a necessary being—a being whose essence involves existence. Put very simply, St Anselm's argument is as follows. We understand by God a being greater than which nothing can be thought. This idea clearly exists in our mind and is the idea of an object with every perfection—every 'positive attribute'. But if the object of this idea were to exist solely in our mind, and not in reality, there would be an idea

23

of something superior to it, namely of the being that possesses not only all the perfections already conceived, but also the additional perfection of real existence. Which is contrary to hypothesis; hence the idea of a most perfect being must correspond to reality. In other words, it is a necessary truth that a most perfect being exists.

The philosophers of the Middle Ages—Christian, Jew and Muslim—were spellbound by such arguments which, for all their abstractness, came to them imbued with their own deepest and most pious emotions. Nor had the spell been broken when Spinoza wrote. Descartes accepted a version of the ontological argument; so did Spinoza; so did the other great rationalist, Leibniz. Indeed, it was not until the eighteenth century, and Kant's decisive refutation, that the argument finally lost its appeal, and by then the medieval vision of man's place in nature had been irrevocably swept away.

The acceptance of the ontological argument, and the resulting conception of a 'necessary being', endowed with omnipotence and omniscience, seems to make nonsense of another theological claim: the claim that man is free, and liable to judgement. If all that exists depends ultimately on the divine nature, and if that nature is governed by necessity, then nothing in the world is contingent. How then is human freedom possible? With the acceptance of the Aristotelian metaphysics, this question—familiar already to the fathers of the Church— acquired a new dimension and a new urgency. Some of the greatest achievements of modern philosophy result from the attempt to reconcile the belief in human freedom with the eternal laws of God's nature, and among these achievements Spinoza's is not only the most imaginative and profound, but perhaps the only one that is truly plausible.

Aristotelian ethics

The influence of Aristotle's *Nicomachean Ethics*, while not at first sight apparent, is as pervasive in Spinoza's writings as the influence of the Aristotelian theology, coming to him, not through the scholastics, but through Jewish and Muslim sources. In order to discover the 'good life for man', Aristotle argued, we must study man's distinguishing attribute—the attribute of reason. A rational being exercises his reason in two distinct ways—theoretically and practically. Happiness comes only through the right exercise of practical reason, so as to fulfil our nature, and not to thwart it. A rational being has not only reason, however, but also emotion. His happiness depends upon his establishing such an order in his emotions as to be led always in the path that reason advises. This in turn can be achieved only by developing certain dispositions of character—the virtues—which lead a man to do and to feel spontaneously that which is in accordance with rational nature.

Spinoza shared Aristotle's view of man as a rational being, whose reason is expressed not only theoretically and practically, but also in his emotional life. He also followed Aristotle in seeing reason as a kind of discipline, which could turn our emotions in the direction of happiness. He departed from Aristotle, however, in his theory of emotion, in his conception of the relation between reason and passion, and in his idea of happiness, of which he gave a Platonic rather than an Aristotelian description.

Grotius and Hobbes

Spinoza's moral system is designed to show us the way to happiness. Spinoza was more of a stoic than Aristotle, more disposed to believe that a man may achieve happiness and peace of mind by his own resources, regardless of his social, political and material circumstances. In a very real sense man, for Spinoza, is his own destiny, and owes his misery and happiness to himself. However, most of mankind neither aspire to the inner freedom of the philosopher, nor live in ways that permit them to understand it. Even so, they may co-exist in peace and harmony, provided only that they are governed by laws suited to their rational nature, and tolerant of their excusable excess.

The Dutch republic, as a sustained experiment in constitutional government, inspired far-reaching speculation concerning the nature of law, freedom and sovereignty. Spinoza was heir to this speculation, and deeply influenced by its greatest exponent Hugo Grotius (Huig de Groot, 1583–1645), author of the first and the greatest treatise of international law (*De Jure Belli ac Pacis*, 1630–35). Grotius recognized that the corruption and decline of Papal jurisdiction, and the birth of the modern state, together gave rise to an urgent need for a form of legality that would transcend the writ of any particular sovereign. The old ideas of government by royal decree were woefully inadequate to man's changed condition. A state, Grotius argued, is an association of free people, joined together in protection of their rights and interests, and all law must stem either from that free association, or from the higher law—the law of nature—which applies to all men, and all nations, in every circumstance of life. The law of nature is eternal and immutable, and binding even on God; to discern it we have but to employ our reason, which leads us as ineluctably to the perception of right and wrong, as it leads us to the truths of logic and mathematics.

Grotius was by no means an isolated thinker; the ideas which he expressed, concerning law, civil association, war and peace, were then current in the Netherlands, and were to elicit an equal interest in England, where Thomas

Hobbes composed his *De Cive* and *Leviathan*, both of which works were studied by Spinoza. Hobbes accepted the broad tenets of natural law, as these had been expounded by Grotius. But natural law, he argued, is totally ineffective without the power that will enforce it. It is therefore power, rather than right, that determines the existence and character of a 'commonwealth'. Power is the common factor in all political arrangements; and its disposition, division and limiting procedure account for the observable differences between governments.

Spinoza's political philosophy is a kind of synthesis of Grotius and Hobbes. Like Grotius, he believes in a natural law, discoverable to reason, that will specify the ideal form of government; but like Hobbes he recognizes no difference in reality between rights and powers, and sees the problem of politics as that of the disposition of power. How, he asks, should power be disposed so that man's rationality might be expressed in it, and his freedom protected by its exercise? His answer to that question is as interesting as anything he wrote.

The Cartesian revolution

It is difficult for us to appreciate the cataclysmic force with which the writings of Descartes struck the Dutch schools, churches and universities, half open as they already were to intellectual innovation. Suffice it to say that, after a period of lively, and often violent controversy, during which the very name of Descartes was for a time declared unmentionable at the University of Leyden, the new philosophy, with its impertinent search for first principles, became accepted as a legitimate, if dangerous, source of theological and scientific argument.

In his *Discours de la Méthode*, 1636 (that it was written in French and not in Latin was an event in itself), Descartes

27

had initiated a programme of radical intellectual reform, refusing to accept as true any proposition which could not be clearly proven. All science, he argued, must be founded in metaphysics, which is itself the system of self-evident truths—truths which do not require further proof than is involved in understanding them. No proposition can be more certain than the premises which are assumed in the proof of it. Unless there are self-evident truths therefore, nothing is knowable, since every judgement will depend, in the last analysis, upon acceptance of unproven premises. Self-evident truths are those whose truth is revealed to the 'natural light' of reason—whose truth, as we should now say, using a term from Grotius, is *a priori*.

Descartes' prime example of a self-evident truth was that contained in the celebrated *cogito*: 'I think, therefore I am'. I cannot doubt that I think, without thereby confirming that I am thinking. (And likewise for the judgement that I exist.) Another example, of more interest to the student of Spinoza, is our knowledge of the validity of an argument. I can see that from the proposition 'p and q' it follows that p, and this too is self-evident. Although the case is different in certain crucial respects from that of the *cogito*, it is nevertheless an instance of a truth revealed to the 'natural light'. Descartes would say that the relation between 'p and q' and 'p' is something that I perceive clearly and distinctly, or something of which I have a 'clear and distinct idea'. Any such idea can be seen to be true by the 'natural light' of reason. 'Clearness and distinctness' were therefore taken by Descartes as providing an intrinsic criterion of truth, a guarantee, contained in the very nature of an idea, that the world is as the idea represents it. Precisely what is meant by 'clear and distinct' is a matter of dispute. A clear idea seems to be one that I comprehend without assistance from the senses or from any source other than my own reasoning powers; a distinct idea one that is unmixed with ideas that are not intrinsic to it. Such an explanation, however, does no more than substitute one obscurity for another. In particular, it employs again the term which most needs explaining—the term 'idea' which Descartes, in common with most of his contemporaries, used to describe any mental content, whatever its individual nature or origin.

Such difficulties were less apparent to the Cartesians than they are to us. The method of 'clear and distinct ideas' was taken to have solved the fundamental problem of knowledge: it seemed to provide the bridge from inner to outer, from the certainty attached to our reasoning, to the world about which we think. Spinoza subscribed to a modified form of Descartes' method, and drew the standard philosophical conclusion. He became convinced that the fundamental premises of human knowledge must be established, not by experience but by reason, since reason alone can provide insight into the essence of things—an essence being precisely that which is captured in a 'clear and distinct idea'. He expressed this point in a letter:

> You ask me if we have need of experience, in order to know if the definition of a given attribute is true. To this I answer that we never need experience, except in cases where the existence of the thing cannot be inferred from its definition . . . (*C* X)

Scientific knowledge, therefore, must begin from self-evident axioms, which treat of essences. And it must proceed therefrom by the method of clear and distinct ideas: in other words, by deduction.

The seventeenth-century philosopher had a paradigm of such a rational science in the geometry of Euclid, which seemed precisely to begin from self-evident premises, and to proceed by chains of clear and distinct reasoning to conclusions which were as compelling and as universally valid as the premises from which they were derived. The ambition therefore arose to generalize the geometric method: that is, to find, for each science, a set of axioms and definitions that would contain the clear and exhaustive statement of its basic postulates. Descartes' own system of physics—rejected by Spinoza on grounds which in some respects anticipate modern scientific thinking—pointed in the direction of such a 'geometrical' exposition. But the exposition itself, Descartes argued, must begin from metaphysics, which is the sole and exclusive domain of first principles.

In his *Principles of Cartesian Philosophy* (1663) Spinoza provided a paradigm of the geometrical method, by reducing Descartes' philosophy to a set of axioms and definitions, and deriving therefrom the main Cartesian conclusions. This exercise, which seemed both to have completed the Cartesian system, and to have shown its fundamental points of error, greatly enhanced the authority of the geometric method. Spinoza's own *Ethics* was therefore conceived entirely in geometric terms, each of its five parts beginning from axioms and definitions and proceeding by mathematical proof towards its conclusions. As the title indicates the book was not intended simply as a treatise of metaphysics. Of equal importance for Spinoza were the problems of human nature, human conduct and human destiny. These too, he believed, could be treated in geometrical fashion, and the resulting answers would have the certainty, necessity and universality of the basic laws of mathematics. His system, therefore, endeavours to move with equal mathematical rigour towards the proposition that 'a substance is prior in nature to its modifications', and towards the proposition that 'there cannot be too much merriment, for it is always good; but on the other hand, melancholy is always bad'. (The proof of the second proposition involves, when traced back to its original axioms, something like 100 steps; this idea of a 'mathematics of laughter' seems less strange, when set beside Spinoza's view that merriment is more easily conceived than observed.)

The design of Spinoza's 'Ethics'

In what follows I shall endeavour to give a summary of the main arguments of Spinoza's *Ethics*. I shall also discuss the political writings, which are more loosely composed and make no pretence at 'geometrical' deduction. In the case of the *Ethics* the geometrical method is an integral part of the book's message; without it, indeed, the very meaning of Spinoza's conclusions would not be fully intelligible. This fact partly explains the fascination exerted by the work. It also presents a formidable obstacle to the modern reader. Not only geometry, but also logic, have undergone profound changes since Spinoza's day, and while mathematicians and scientists continue to make use of the 'axiomatic method', they are no longer so disposed to believe that the axioms of any science are 'self-evident', or that the 'ideas' necessary to a science may carry some intrinsic mark of truth. Spinoza was himself aware of a major obstacle to that last suggestion, namely, that a set of axioms and definitions is composed not of ideas (whatever they may be) but of words, and no word bears its meaning on its face. Only in the context of the system as a whole can the content of any axiom be specified. But how can we guarantee that there is only one consistent interpretation of the system, or that this interpretation will be understood by the enlightened reader?

Moses Maimonides repeatedly cautions his readers against the 'language of man'—the everyday language in which philosophical questions must perforce be discussed, but which can be used only figuratively in the expression of ultimate truth. His *Guide to the Perplexed* is as much a treatise on metaphor and its dangers as an exposition of monotheistic metaphysics. Spinoza follows Maimonides in rejecting the ordinary meanings which attach to words, and in asking his readers to attend, not to language, but to the 'ideas' which he is attempting to convey by means of it. Common usage is governed by the imagination, which associates words, not with clear and distinct ideas, but with the confused conceptions of experience. In the language of imagination nothing can be truly described, and nothing is more misleadingly rendered by the imagination than the ultimate subject-matter of philosophical speculation—God himself: 'Words are formed according to popular fancy and understanding [*ad libitum et ad captum vulgi*], and are therefore signs of things only as they are in the imagination, and not as they are in the intellect . . .' (*I* xi).

The Latin of the *Ethics* is a technical language, to be understood only in the full elaboration of the proofs. Such a language may be as easily misinterpreted as any other: indeed, more easily. In reply to questions from Simon de Vries, Spinoza explains (*C* IX) that it is possible to use language to gain access to the realm of eternal truth, provided that one takes care to present only *real* definitions: definitions which are not arbitrary stipulations, but which present the essence of the thing defined. To suppose that such definitions are possible, however, is already to assume one of the major claims of Spinoza's metaphysics—a claim which he establishes only by proofs in which 'real definitions' are employed.

It would take us too far afield to explore this difficulty in its entirety. It is one which Descartes too had encountered, and which was to be encountered by many of Spinoza's successors. Suffice it to say that the reader can never be truly certain, in studying the *Ethics*, that he has really advanced from the words on the page to the 'ideas' that are expressed in them. Often he will seem to grasp the whole system in its clarity: like the towers of Valhalla, however, the vision comes only with the gathering of darkness, and is no sooner granted than at once extinguished by the night.

The *Ethics* consists of five parts. The first, 'Concerning God', outlines Spinoza's version of the ontological argument, and his theory that God is not distinct from the world, but immanent within it. The second, 'Concerning the nature and origin of the mind', contains a succinct and fascinating summary of Spinoza's physics, while principally addressing itself to the major problem of Cartesian philosophy: that of the relation between mind and matter. Descartes had argued that mind is a separate substance from matter; at the same time, his conception of substance implied (as he recognized, and as Spinoza proved) that there can be no interaction between substances. In which case what place has man in nature, and how is knowledge possible? Spinoza answers those questions, but by rejecting Descartes' premises. The third part, 'On the origin and nature of the emotions', contains Spinoza's account of human nature, and his answer to the major difficulty raised by his own metaphysics: the question of individual existence. If everything that exists exists in God, in what sense does the world contain individual things, and in what sense am *I* an individual, with a nature and destiny that are mine? Part Four concerns 'Human servitude and the strength of the emotions'. Here Spinoza describes the enslaved condition of humanity, compelled by passion, opinion and imagination to deny its true nature, and yet at at the same time expressing, even in its bondage, the absolute perfection of the universe of which it is a component. In the final part, Spinoza describes 'The power of the intellect or human freedom', showing how man may achieve freedom and happiness through the exercise of reason, and how, in doing so, he aspires to that absolute knowledge of the world which is the blessedness of God.

3 God

In the first part of the *Ethics* Spinoza addresses himself to the question 'What exists?'—and his answer is contained in Propositions 14 and 15: 'Except God no substance can be granted or conceived', and 'Whatever is, is in God, and nothing can exist or be conceived without God'. Those striking pronouncements are less clear—and, when interpreted, marginally less surprising—than they seem. The terms 'God', 'substance', 'conceive' and 'in' are all technicalities of Spinoza's philosophy, and their interpretation is a matter of dispute. In Part 1 of the *Ethics* they derive their sense largely from an elaborate version of the ontological argument for the existence of God.

The ontological argument seems to prove the existence of something from the conception of that thing. It provides a paradigm of rationalist philosophy, beginning from a 'clear and distinct idea' of God, and leading, by 'clear and distinct' steps, to a conclusion about the world: namely that God exists, and exists necessarily. Whereas previous philosophers had taken the ontological argument to show that at least one thing (God) exists, Spinoza believes the argument also to show that *at most* one thing exists, and hence that everything which exists is, in some sense, 'in' God. The major difficulty in understanding this conclusion derives from the little word 'in'. Spinoza's use of this word owes its sense partly to his peculiar appreciation, and idiosyncratic revision, of the distinction between substance and attribute, and partly to a premise that is so deeply concealed in Spinoza's philosophy as to remain unacknowledged throughout the first part of the *Ethics*.

The hidden assumption

The hidden assumption of Spinoza's philosophy is that reality and conception *coincide*, so that relations between ideas correspond exactly to relations in reality. At a later point, Spinoza purports to prove this thesis, and to provide a theory of knowledge that will justify his own special version of the method of 'clear and distinct ideas'. But since that method (or something like it) is assumed in the very proof of it, the hidden assumption remains, in the end, no more than an assumption.

Certain consequences are already manifest in the axioms of the first part of the *Ethics*. Thus Spinoza asserts (Axiom 4) that 'the knowledge (*cognitio*) of an effect depends upon the knowledge of its cause, and involves the same'. For Spinoza, to say that A causes B is to say that B is dependent on A for its existence and nature. This dependence between things is 'expressed in' or 'conceived through' a dependence between ideas. The idea of B is dependent on the idea of A if its truth must be established by reference to the idea of A. The conclusions of a mathematical proof are therefore *dependent* on the premises. Mathematical reasoning is indeed a paradigm of the relation of 'rational dependence' between ideas. It is also a paradigm of 'causality', which is the relation that exists between A and B when the existence and nature of B must be explained in terms of A. Through proof we *explain* a conclusion, and if the premises are self-evident, we explain it completely.

The hidden assumption implies that relations of dependence in the world are all intelligible as logical relations between ideas. Thus something is independent if its properties follow from its idea: i.e. if you do not need to look outside the idea of the thing in order to explain it. B is dependent on A if the nature of B follows not from the idea of B but from the idea of A. All properties are in this sense dependent on, or caused by, the substances in which they inhere. And this is what Spinoza means by 'in': 'B is *in* A' is another way of saying that A is the explanation of B.

An empiricist would object strongly to this aspect of Spinoza's philosophy, arguing that Spinoza has detached causality from the world and attached it instead to our conceptions. But what guarantee do we have that the world *is* as we conceive it? Spinoza would have answered such an objection by referring again to the method of 'clear and distinct ideas', which presents our paradigm of knowledge. Nothing can be more certain that the self-evident premises from which reason begins, and if these do not provide a guarantee of truth then nothing does. But a self-evident truth is precisely one in which the passage from thought to reality is accomplished: we perceive from the very idea that the world is as the idea represents it to be. In a self-evident idea we have a complete and satisfactory answer to the question 'why?'. Through such ideas the world explains itself to us. In his axioms, therefore, Spinoza can employ the notion of 'conception', and still believe that he provides, by means of it, a description of things in the world.

However, the axioms are far from self-evident, and derive their claim to be 'adequate' only in the course of proofs which already assume them to be so. Spinoza, aware of this difficulty, attempted to provide a method for the 'improvement of the understanding' which would lead us, of its own accord, to knowledge. (*I, passim.*) But this method does little to sustain Spinoza's hidden assumption, that the world really is intelligible to reason, and that its causality really is a 'causality of reason'. Throughout the proofs of the *Ethics*, therefore, the reader can never be certain whether the extraordinary ideas which are brought so compellingly before him are fiction or reality.

Substance, mode, and attribute

Spinoza begins with the following definition, taken from Maimonides: 'I understand that to be cause of itself [*causa sui*] whose essence involves existence and whose nature cannot be conceived unless existing' (*E* 1, Definition 1). That definition, it transpires, identifies the whole subject-matter of the *Ethics*, and also the entire contents of the world. It is followed by a tri-partite distinction between 'substance', 'attribute' and 'mode'.

Substance is 'that which is in itself and is conceived through itself', that, the conception of which does not require the conception of some other thing (*E* 1, Definition 3). In other words, substance is something of which we can obtain an 'adequate idea', through which its nature can be understood without recourse to anything outside of it. Spinoza argues (*E* 1, 6) that whatever is, in this way, conceptually independent, is also *ontologically* independent, depending for its existence on nothing outside itself. Hence 'existence appertains to the nature of substance' (*E* 1, 7), and every substance contains within itself the complete explanation of it own nature and existence. In that case substance is necessarily 'cause of itself': its essence involves existence, and it cannot therefore be conceived except as existing. The first answer to the riddle of existence, therefore, is that *substance* exists, and exists necessarily.

It is already obvious that Spinoza's use of the term 'substance' does not conform to the Aristotelian tradition. At the same time, Spinoza regarded his proofs as deriving the inescapable logical consequences of an idea which had previously been only confusedly understood. Many scholastic and Cartesian thinkers had assumed substances to be the ultimate constituents of reality, and, as such, self-dependent. What they had failed to see was the consequence of these assumptions—namely, that any substance must be *causa sui*, and therefore necessarily existent.

The traditional distinction between substance and attribute is redescribed by Spinoza as the distinction between substance and *modification* or *mode* (*modus*). (The term 'attribute' he employs in another—and wholly peculiar—way.) A mode is something which cannot exist independently but only *in* some other thing, upon which it depends. In his earlier writings Spinoza repeatedly affirms the principle that, except for substances and modes, nothing exists (*M* Pt 1, Ch. 1; Pt 2, Ch. 1; *C* XII). However, he does not confine modes to the logical category of properties and relations: modes include individual things. You and I are both modes of the divine substance, since we can both be conceived as not existing, and therefore owe the explanation of our existence to something outside ourselves. Hence we are not self-dependent, and if we exist, it is through the power of something outside of us. On this definition, the category of mode is extremely wide: it includes (in common parlance) properties (the redness of this book); relations (this book's being smaller than others); facts (that this book exists); processes (this book's slow disintegration); and individuals (the book itself). The distinctions between those categories are all insignificant for Spinoza: so far have we already come from 'the language of man'! Spinoza does, however, distinguish 'finite' from 'infinite modes', the later being modifications of substance which are manifest in every finite mode. (Spinoza's two examples—'motion and rest' and 'the face of the whole universe'—form the basis of his physics, which I discuss below.)

This part of Spinoza's philosophy can best be summarized in his own words:

> When I say that I mean by substance that which is conceived through and in itself; and that I mean by modification or accident that which is in something else, and is conceived through that wherein it is, evidently it follows that substance is by nature prior to its accidents. For without the former the latter can neither be nor be conceived. Secondly it follows that besides substances and accidents nothing exists really or externally to the intellect.   (*C* IV)

Once we understand the use of the word 'in', to denote the relation of rational dependence, such passages present no special difficulty, even to a reader who rejects their hidden assumption.

The greatest single obstacle to an understanding of Spinoza's philosophy is that presented by the term 'attribute'. An attribute is defined as 'that which the intellect perceives as constituting the essence of substance' (*E* 1, Definition 4), and there are several—possibly infinitely many—'attributes'. At the same time, an attribute is not simply a subjective aspect—a way things seem from a particular point of view. For, by the hidden assumption, 'what the intellect perceives as constituting the essence of substance' really *does* constitute the essence of substance. Hence the assertion that a substance has two or more attributes is tantamount to the assertion that its essence can be conceptualized in two independent ways: and this is an extremely puzzling idea. On this view, two people can each have complete knowledge of the fundamental nature of a thing, and yet each give completely incommensurable accounts of it.

Some light is cast on Spinoza's theory by an argument that provided him with a paradigm of philosophical deduction. In a famous passage of the *Meditations* Descartes had reasoned as follows: Consider a lump of wax: it has a certain shape, size, colour, odour—in short a set of 'sensory qualities', perceivable to sight, touch, taste and smell. But when I approach the wax to the fire I find that its colour, shape, hardness, odour—all those qualities in terms of which I distinguish it—undergo a change. And yet the wax remains: no constituent of reality is destroyed in this transformation. It follows, Descartes argued, that the wax possesses its sensory qualities only accidentally—they are not 'of its nature' or 'essential'.

The sensory qualities of such an object are therefore no more than passing accidents, through which its essence is dimly and confusedly perceived. If we are to know the essence of the wax we must consult not the senses but the intellect, which is alone capable of grasping the essences of things. The only properties that the wax seems to have essentially are extension, flexibility and movability in space. From this we may conclude that material substances (such as the wax) are essentially extended, and that changes in material substances are changes in their spatial disposition. This conclusion gives us the first principle of physical science, and Descartes was further confirmed in it by his interpretation of Euclidean geometry. For it seemed as though Euclid had shown that we have a 'clear and distinct idea' of space, and therefore can reach knowledge of all its properties by reason alone, through a deductive science that makes no reference to sensory experience. It remains only to complete that science, by a similar deductive exposition of the properties of an 'occupant' of space: that whose essence is to be *in* space,

41

and changeable with respect to space; whose essence is that of an 'extended thing'.

This paradigm of rationalist philosophy underlies Spinoza's theory of the attributes, of which extension is one. Things in space can be understood *a priori*, and their nature disclosed to reason, precisely because extension constitutes the essence of whatever possesses it. By conceiving extension the intellect is acquainted with a 'real essence', existing independently of the finite mind which conceives it. The intellect is granted a complete insight into the nature of something—an insight from which the fundamental properties of extended things may eventually be deduced. An attribute is that which is 'attributed' to reality by the intellect, in the course of such a complete and systematic conception. To say that there are two attributes is to say that we can know the world completely in two incommensurable ways.

The ontological argument

Spinoza defines God as 'a substance consisting of infinite attributes, each of which expresses eternal and infinite essence', and argues that, since no 'cause or reason' could possibly be granted which could *prevent* the existence of such a being, it follows that God necessarily exists. Since it is in the nature of God to exist, God must exist unless prevented, but he cannot be prevented.

As Spinoza is aware, the same could be said of any substance, since a substance is that which contains within itself (within its idea) the complete explanation of its own existence. A substance is whatever is shown to exist by an ontological argument. That which owes its existence to an 'external cause' is of necessity not a substance but a mode. Substance, moreover, is always 'infinite in its own kind'— i.e. unlimited by anything of the same nature as itself. (For to be limited is to be affected by an 'external cause'.) Hence every substance exists necessarily and infinitely.

The hidden premise of rationalism led Spinoza to the conclusion that there is only one substance. For while we can explain the existence of *one* substance from the nature of that substance, no such *a priori* explanation could be given, he believed, for the existence of *more* than one substance of the same kind: 'all things which are conceived to exist in the plural must necessarily be produced by external causes, and not by the force of their own nature' (*C* XXIV). And if some substance existed of another kind— one that lacked God's infinite perfections—it would necessarily owe its existence *to* God, and therefore be a mode of God and not a substance at all. (It would be a *limitation* of God's nature, that something existed of which his nature was not the ultimate explanation: but by hypothesis God is unlimited.)

No other substance but God can therefore be granted. Nor, adds Spinoza (*E* 1, 14), can such another substance even be conceived, since to conceive of a substance is to conceive of it as existing (each substance being *causa sui*), and therefore—by the ontological argument—to establish its existence. Hence 'Whatever is, is in God, and nothing can exist or be conceived without God'. Once we understand the technical sense of the words 'in' and 'conceived' in this proposition, its conclusion seems inescapable, and Spinoza's proofs—far more complex than I have been able to display—satisfied him that this proposition contains the complete and only answer to the riddle of existence.

Not every rationalist who accepted the ontological argument also embraced Spinoza's monistic conclusion. Leibniz, for example, endeavoured to reconcile the rationalist assumption with a pluralistic theory of the universe, admitting an infinity of substances besides God into that 'best of all possible worlds' which is the actual world of God's creation. But, as Leibniz acknowledged, there could be no interaction between these separate substances, no dependence of one on the other, no explanation of their seeming responsiveness one to another, and indeed, no real relation between them at all. And the picture of a universe of infinitely many wholly unrelated substances is at least as hard to understand as the monism of Spinoza, and far less easy to reconcile with appearances.

One qualification should be mentioned. Spinoza often cautions us against speaking of God's 'singleness'. To call him 'one or single' is to imply that God might be enumerated—as though, counting the elements of the universe, we stop at the number one (*C* L). Number, however, does not pertain to the essence of things: it belongs, rather, to our finite understanding of them, and cannot feature in any *a priori* exposition of their nature. The origin of this thought is in Moses Maimonides (*Guide to the Perplexed*, i, 51–7), who argued that number belongs to the 'language of man', and can therefore be applied only negatively to God. But Spinoza went further than Maimonides, and based upon this and similar observations a peculiar and influential philosophy of arithmetic, according to which number signifies, not some property of reality, but a feature of human perception. Of this philosophy I shall have more to say below.

The attributes of God

An attribute is given by a 'complete and adequate idea' of God, one which, because of its 'adequacy', shows God as he essentially is. An attribute is, therefore, more than an essential property. I am an animal, and also a person: if I lose either of those properties, I cease to exist, and therefore each property is essential. But neither 'constitutes my essence' in the way that an attribute constitutes the essence of God. It is extremely difficult to understand how God can have more than one attribute: i.e. how his essence can be completely constituted in several incommensurable ways.

Spinoza identifies two attributes of God: thought and extension. The first is the system of ideas, the second that of physical objects. Our physical science is not a deductive system, but a series of generalizations based in observation of 'finite modes'. Nevertheless, our very procedure, in deriving therefrom a lawlike description of the 'infinite modes', presupposes the possibility of a deductive science. Such a science of 'extension' would provide complete knowledge of a self-dependent totality. From its self-evident premises, by deductive argument, a description of the world could be elaborated, in which all the relations of dependence (the 'causal laws') would be identified. The physical (extended) world must therefore have the character of a self-sufficient system, beyond which we do not have to enquire in order to explain any physical occurrence. An ideal science of the physical (of extension) would give us knowledge of an essence, and therefore of the substance in which that essence resides. It follows that extension is an attribute of God.

Descartes, like Spinoza, saw the physical world as a single and substantial system. However, he was unable to account for the place of mind within it. Our mental states (ideas) seem to be linked to the physical world by causal connections, without being modifications of any physical substance. They are, Descartes argued, essentially non-physical, without place, shape, boundaries or movement. However, only if A and B are modifications of a single substance can there be a causal relation between them. What, then, is the relation of the mind to the body?

Descartes fudged this issue, and it proved to be the major reason for dissatisfaction with the Cartesian system. Spinoza solved the problem in his own remarkable way, by arguing that ideas and physical objects are modifications of a single substance, conceived, however, in two separate and incommensurable ways, now as mind, now as matter or extension. In referring to ideas we are referring to God through another of his attributes, and intimating another complete and *a priori* science of the whole. The clear and indubitable apprehension that we have of the nature of individual ideas suggests that an *a priori* science of the mental (of reality conceived in mental terms) is as real a possibility as an *a priori* science of the physical (of reality conceived as extension).

Two new problems are raised by Spinoza's ingenious solution. First, how many attributes does God have? Secondly, what precisely does it mean to say that God has more than one attribute, and how is this compatible with Spinoza's theory that reality is one? The second of those problems will occupy us in the next chapter. The first, however, requires an answer here.

Spinoza defines God as a 'substance consisting of infinite attributes, each of which expresses eternal and infinite essence' (*E* 1, 11). The definition is repeated in various forms in the correspondence (e.g. *C* II), but never in such a way as to suggest that Spinoza did not mean, by the first occurrence of 'infinite', 'infinitely many'. And yet he refers to only two such attributes. Commentators are therefore divided as to the meaning of Spinoza's definition. Does he really mean that there are infinitely many attributes, or only that each attribute is in some sense infinite in its own nature? (*S* 19 and 34 point unambiguously to the first interpretation as does *E* 1, 9.) Spinoza upholds the first interpretation in correspondence with Tschirnhaus, but in terms that are so obscure as perhaps to justify the misgivings of the learned. He affirms (*C* LXIV) that there are infinitely many attributes, but argues that the human mind—which is (see below) the idea of the human body—can know only two, extension (revealed in the body) and thought (revealed in the idea of it). But the explanation is neither intelligible nor obviously sincere.

In the nature of the case, Spinoza's mode of argument cannot generate numerical conclusions: he can establish that there is *one* thing of a kind, or that there are *infinite* things of a kind, or that there are none (cf. *E* 1, 8, Scholium 2). But this is because 'one', 'infinite' and 'none' denote, for Spinoza, not numbers, but ontological categories: independent existence, 'unlimitedness' and non-existence. It is therefore impossible that there should be an *a priori* proof of the fact that there are just two attributes. At the same time 'infinite' must be compatible with 'at least two' if Spinoza is to argue as he does: 'infinite' must therefore sustain *some* kind of numerical interpretation. Again, however, Spinoza argues as though number is not in the nature of things, but imposed upon them by our imagination (see below).

Here, then, is an issue which presents formidable difficulties to Spinoza. And here it is Spinoza's turn to fudge, both in the letter to Tschirnhaus, and in his wider use of the concept of infinity. Moreover, not only does his system contain this great and disconcerting lacuna. The attempt by commentators to fill it has produced one of the most exasperating, tedious and futile secondary literatures in the entire history of scholarship. I therefore say no more about the problem, except that it is insoluble.

God or Nature

It follows from Spinoza's theory that God is not distinct from the world but identical with it. But God is conceived by the human mind in two separate ways: when contemplating the divine mind, and our own mind as part of it, or equally when investigating the structure of the physical world, we are advancing our knowledge of God. All that is done for the sake of that knowledge is well done, and done to our salvation.

Spinoza expresses his monism in a celebrated phrase; the world is *Deus sive Natura*—'God or Nature'. This pronouncement has caused Spinoza to be considered both as an atheist and as a pantheist, even—in the famous words of Novalis—as a 'God-intoxicated man', for whom the divine countenance shines forth from the whole of nature. Both interpretations would have been repudiated by Spinoza, as displaying a limited understanding of God. His theology is essentially impersonal, just as his conception of the physical world is essentially theological. All causality obeys a logical paradigm, and all explanation is really a form of proof. To understand the causality of things, therefore, is to understand a complex mental operation, undertaken by an infinite mind.

Various consequences follow. First, God is not the 'transeunt' but the 'immanent' cause of everything: that is, he exists *in* the world of his creation, and not beyond it (*E* 1, 18, and *S* 30, 34 and 36ff.). Moreover, since causality is a form of necessity, and since the divine nature is eternally and necessarily as it is, everything that happens in the world happens by necessity. There is as little freedom in the physical world as in the world of ideas, and an effect follows from its cause with the rigid necessity of a mathematical proof. Moreover, every human action, as a mode of God, arises out of the same unbreakable chain of necessity, and therefore ideas such as 'chance' and 'freedom' cannot be given the significance that they have in the imaginations of the vulgar. Things could have been otherwise only if God could have been otherwise (*S* 44): but that is to suppose the possibility of another substance, and such a supposition is strictly incoherent.

Those conclusions are already counter-intuitive. But matters are worse than they imply. For there is a real sense in which nothing in Spinoza's world really 'happens'. God is, indeed, the cause of everything, but he is the 'eternal' cause. He does not, rightly conceived, participate in change. He is not 'in' time, and the conception of time plays no part in the true knowledge of God. While we understand the world in terms of 'change' and 'process', these descriptions attach only to modes of God, and not to the divine essence. They express only the partial and confused perception of those who have no complete or adequate idea of the world. We can indeed use these partial perceptions, in conjunction with a proper scientific method, to derive an account of the 'infinite modes' of God. And in doing so we provide a fuller explanation of the world than any that is evident to common sense. Nevertheless, to explain things ultimately we must not relate them to what precedes them in time—since that is merely to relate one mode to another; rather, we must show their timeless relation to the eternal essence of God. An ideal science, therefore, like a true religion, would aim to see the world not in its temporal dimension, but 'under the aspect of eternity' (*sub specie aeternitatis*), in the manner of a mathematical proof.

God is the only 'free' cause, since he alone is self-creating. In so far as we think of God in this way we understand nature as an active and creative principle, intelligible in and through itself—as *natura naturans*, to use Spinoza's scholastic phrase. But we can also study nature as the product of creation, as the working out of a creative endeavour through the infinite and finite modes of the one true substance: as *natura naturata* (*E* 1, 29, Scholium). There is no contradiction between these two ideas; each approaches the one identical reality, from two contrasting points of view. The philosopher and the scientist emphasize different features of the world, follow different interests and inspire different passions in the soul. But the aim of their study is in each case the same: the supreme good which consists in the adequate knowledge of God (see especially *S* Chs. 8 and 9).

This, then, is the conclusion to which Spinoza's metaphysics tends: Nothing exists save the one substance—the self-contained, self-sustaining, and self-explanatory system which constitutes the world. This system may be understood in many ways: as God or Nature; as mind or matter; as creator or created; as eternal or temporal. It can be known adequately and clearly through its attributes, partially and confusedly through its modes. And to understand it in its totality, under the aspect of eternity, is also to know that everything in the world exists by necessity, and that it could not be other than it is.

The interpretation of Spinoza's metaphysics

Spinoza detaches the conception of substance from its intellectual origins. A substance is no longer, in his writings, an 'individual object', or the normal subject-matter of thought. God is not 'individuated' by his true description, since it is impossible to conceive of any other entity from which he could be distinguished. It is perhaps easier to understand 'substance' in the terms set by the new science of the seventeenth century, in which quantity and transformation take precedence over quality and classification. As I remarked in the last chapter, we identify the contents of the world not only as individual things but also as stuffs ('substances' in our more usual modern understanding of the term). There is a modern equivalent of Spinoza's monism in the view that all transformations in the world are transformations of a single stuff—matter for the Newtonians, energy for the followers of Planck and Einstein. Spinoza himself is sometimes thought to be nearer to Einstein, in taking 'motion and rest' as the fundamental variable, and in arguing that 'bodies are distinguished from each other in respect of the motion and rest contained in them' (*E* 2, 13). However, this 'motion and rest' is not, for Spinoza, an attribute of substance, but an 'infinite mode': in other words, something which everywhere inheres in, but is not exhaustive of, the ultimate reality. At the same time, extension (the attribute) can be seen as a 'power to produce motion and rest' (*S*, 120).

The ideas of God's unity and self-generation also have their equivalents in modern science, being tantamount, on the interpretation just ventured, to the views: (1) that all objects in the world are in thoroughgoing causal interaction; (2) that the universe is a closed system, beyond which we cannot search (and, given the truth of (1), beyond which we need not search) for the cause of anything within it. There is no answer to the question 'why?' that does not refer to the actual system of the world, and the attempt to go beyond that system—to find a 'transcendental causality' of created things—is inherently meaningless. A single stuff, obedient to a single set of laws definitive of its nature, gives rise to all that we observe. The task of science is to provide the complete description of that substance and the laws which apply to it, so that every event can be finally explained. Moreover, descriptions of the substance and descriptions of the laws which govern it are not two descriptions but one: to give the ultimate properties of extension (matter, energy) is at the same time to give the laws which govern all extended things.

Such a 'translation' of Spinoza's theology has met with a certain approval among contemporary commentators; partly because it renders the rest of Spinoza's philosophy useful as a morality for scientific man. At first sight it is far from the vision of the 'God-intoxicated' pantheist which stirred the sympathies of Novalis and Goethe. But perhaps only at first sight. We should remember the calm religious faith which Einstein built upon his theory of relativity—a theory which began precisely from the assumptions that I have just outlined, and which seemed, to its inventor, to justify the ways of God to man.

The real difficulty for the interpretation is suggested, however, by the comparison with Einstein. Space, time and number lie at the foundation of modern physics; but, what are they for Spinoza? Time in particular seems little better than a metaphor, a kind of pervasive figure of speech which runs through all our experience, but only because our experience is an 'inadequate' guide to ultimate reality. Before returning to that difficulty, however, we must face what was for Spinoza the most important of all the problems raised by his metaphysics: the problem of man's place in nature.

4 Man

Spinoza's answer to the riddle of existence can be put succinctly: all things that exist, exist necessarily, in thoroughgoing interdependence. The ensuing metaphysics has certain disturbing implications for man's self-understanding. Mentality may, in some sense, be a distinguishing feature of people: nevertheless, everything in the world is expressible both as idea and as physical object, and the relation between ideas and extended things is made not more but less easy to grasp, by Spinoza's theory of the attributes. Furthermore, Spinoza's monism generates a highly paradoxical idea of the human person. The individual person is not, it seems, an individual at all. Nor is anything else. The identity, separateness, and self-sufficiency of the person all seem to be denied by Spinoza, and man, as part of nature, seems to be no more important a feature in the scheme of things than are rocks and stones and trees.

Finally, the assertion that everything happens by necessity seems to leave the whole of morality in doubt. It is unclear whether the question 'What shall I do?' has any meaning for Spinoza. For not only does the 'I' seem to be problematic—a fleeting mode of God with neither individuality not self-dependence—the whole suggestion that such a thing might actually *do* something is without meaning, since in nothing does it have the slightest choice.

The most original part of Spinoza's philosophy consists in his attempt to answer the three problems that we have sketched—the problem of mind and body, the problem of individual existence, and the problem of freedom—and in doing so, to reconcile the quest for happiness with the knowledge of God. Nor is this attempt without importance for us, who are as beset as was Spinoza by a sense of man's fleetingness, fragility and metaphysical nullity, and above all by a sense of his utter dependence upon a totality which he does not control.

Attributes and aspects

We know God both through the attribute of extension and through the attribute of thought. The temptation is to interpret this theory 'subjectively'—i.e. to suppose that Spinoza is describing two ways of perceiving a single reality, rather than an intrinsic duality in the reality perceived. Spinoza himself encourages such an interpretation:

> You desire, though there is no need, that I should illustrate by an example, how one and the same thing can be stamped with two names. In order not to seem miserly, I will give you two. First, I say that by Israel is meant the third patriarch; I mean the same by Jacob, the name Jacob having been given, because the patriarch in question had caught hold of the heel of his brother. Secondly, by a colourless surface I mean a surface, which reflects all rays of light without altering them. I mean the same by a white surface, with this difference, that a surface is called white in reference to a man looking at it. (*C* IX)

Neither of Spinoza's examples has any obvious bearing on the problem of the attributes (each of which is supposed to provide a complete and identifying *essence* of the thing to which it is attributed); and each example is obscure. But both seem to encourage the interpretation of the attributes as 'perspectives' or 'aspects'. We can look on God, now under the aspect of thought, now under the aspect of extension, rather as a man may look at a picture, first as a disposition of coloured patches, then as a portrait, and in each case be understanding the same material thing.

Such an interpretation neglects Spinoza's hidden assumption. The rationalist sees our knowledge of the world on the model of mathematics. Just as there is no gap between how numbers are, and how they are represented by our proofs, so, for the rationalist, is there no gap between how the world is, and how it is represented in our reasoning—provided that we reason, as in mathematics, by 'clear and distinct ideas'. This feature of mathematics is often taken by empiricists to show that mathematical entities, such as numbers, are not really independent of us: if we can know all about them, if their properties perfectly mirror our cognition of them, then this is because they are in some sense *constructed* in the act of understanding them. For the rationalist, however, mathematics is simply the perfect illustration of the possibility that I may gain *a priori* knowledge of something which is not myself. Similarly Spinoza defines an attribute as that which the intellect perceives to be the essence of a substance. And what the intellect (properly schooled) perceives to be the essence of something, *is* the essence of that thing. The two conceptions are therefore not two points of view on the world, but two complete and adequate descriptions of the world as it essentially is, and an attribute is not truly distinct from the substance in which it inheres. In earlier writings Spinoza put the point as follows: 'Being as being, by itself alone, as substance, does not affect us, and therefore it is to be explained by some attribute, from which it is yet not distinguished, save ideally' (*M* Pt 1, Ch. 3). At the same time, an attribute is so called because 'the intellect *attributes* a certain nature to substance' (*C* IX).

Perhaps the best way of understanding Spinoza's thought is in terms of an analogy put forward by Thomas Carson Mark (see Bibliography). Consider Spinoza's paradigm of objective science: the geometry of Euclid. The axioms put forward by Euclid employ intuitive notions of the plane figure, such as line and point, which we have no difficulty in relating to our everyday experience of space. The same axioms can be re-expressed using Cartesian coordinates, which show how figures are determined by equations of two variables, and which transform the resulting proofs of geometrical theorems into proofs in algebra. The proofs correspond to each other, and neither science delivers results that are not delivered in equivalent form by the other. But there would be a strange fault of logic exhibited by anyone who changed from one idiom to the other in the course of a proof. Here one might say that the Cartesian and Euclidean presentations of plane geometry give complete accounts of the same system of mathematical truths, and a complete analysis of all the relations of logical dependence that obtain within the system. At the same time, the propositions of one science, even though necessarily true, cannot be substituted in the proofs belonging to the other. Any proposition that is less than a conception of the whole is marked indelibly as *either* Cartesian *or* Euclidean, and only the whole (or, in Spinoza's words, 'adequate') idea which is the total science would show the subject-matter to be in each case one and the same.

The analogy is less than perfect. But it is probably as near as we can come to providing a model for Spinoza's theory of the relation between the attributes of thought and extension, each of which provides complete and adequate knowledge of the essence of a single substance. Thought and extension each represent reality as it essentially is, and each attribute gives a *complete* account of that reality. Hence every mode—including every object in the system of time and change—can be described both in mental and in physical terms, and if we are not acquainted with the ideas which express the reality of a stone or a table, this is merely a result of our confused perception. In our own case, however, we know both the mental and the physical expression of a single finite mode. The mind, Spinoza tells us, is a particular *idea*, namely 'the idea of the body' (*E* 2, 13). This idea is 'not simple, but composed of many ideas' (*E* 2, 15), and to each of its components there corresponds a bodily process which is its 'object' or *ideatum*.

Normally, when we say that an idea is an idea *of* some object, we do not mean to suggest that the idea and the object are intimately connected. After all, we have ideas of distant objects which cannot exist in the human mind, and ideas of fictions, which do not exist at all. Normally the word 'of' means 'about', and the 'object' of an idea is that which is represented in or through it. For Spinoza, however, that way of thinking is merely a reflection of our own inadequate understanding. The only *real* cognitive relation that could exist between an idea and a material thing, is the relation that exists between an idea, which is a mode of the single substance conceived under the attribute of thought, and the very same mode conceived under the attribute of extension. Whether we can call this relation one of identity is a nice point of logic. Nevertheless, Spinoza affirms that 'the mind and the body are one and the same thing, which is conceived now under the attribute of thought, now under the attribute of extension' (*E* 2, 21, Scholium).

What, then, *is* the relation between mind and body? This is again a point of scholarly controversy, but we may abbreviate a vast and inconclusive literature into a short and probably equally satisfactory sentence, by saying that

Spinoza combined ontological monism with conceptual dualism. Mind and body are one *thing*; but to describe that thing as mind and to describe it as body are to situate it within two separate and incommensurable systems. The details of those systems cannot be mutually substituted, and therefore the assertion of a causal relation (a relation of dependence) between mind and body is incoherent. If we mean by 'a is identical to b' that 'a' can be truly and sensibly substituted for 'b' in any true sentence about b, then mind and body are not identical. On the other hand, the complete system to which the mind belongs is precisely the same system as that to which the body belongs. Moreover, mind and body occur at isomorphic points in the two parallel systems. Ontologically speaking, therefore, the mind is 'nothing but' the body, and has no reality apart from the reality attributed to the body, even though 'the body cannot determine the mind to think, nor the mind the body to remain in motion or at rest' (*E* 3, 2).

Such a view of the relation between mind and body is not without its modern adherents. Many philosophers now argue as follows (from premises which mirror the 'scientific' interpretation that I gave of Spinoza's metaphysics): To describe the behaviour of a person in mental terms is not to refer to some occult process lying beyond the transformations of the body, but to describe those very transformations, using concepts of a radically different kind from those employed in the natural sciences. A man who thinks, desires, or rages is in a certain physical condition, and this condition constitutes, in some manner, his thought, desire or rage. But in describing his condition in mental terms, we use concepts that have no place in the scientific explanation of nature: we are *interpreting* his behaviour, by situating it in the 'human world' of personal intercourse. A critic, describing the meaning of a piece of music, is describing the very same objects as the physicist, who describes its component sounds; and yet he is interpreting them in a way that has a special significance for those who respond to music. The meaning of the music is not separate from the sounds: rather it *is* the sounds, understood through conceptions that place them in significant relation with ourselves. In a similar way, the mind of another is not separate from the bodily processes which cause his behaviour, even though, when we see them as mind, we see them under a special interpretation, which relates them to our own response. This interpretation employs concepts that could play no role in the formulation of scientific laws. Hence the assertion of a causal relation between physical and mental events is inherently paradoxical, perhaps even incoherent.

Individuals and 'conatus'

As so far presented, however, the theory is radically incomplete. For it tells us only of the relation in the abstract of the mental to the physical. It gives us no account of the particularity of the human mind, and no idea of how we might individuate, either the mind, or the body which is its *ideatum*. And without individuation the relation between mind and body is still in doubt. How, then, can we understand the separateness and individuality that is (in such cases) attributed to finite modes?

It is only in a problematic sense that God can be spoken of as an individual—as 'one or single'. And indeed, it might be supposed that there is really no place in Spinoza's philosophy for the concept of an individual, or for the distinction, so important to our ordinary thought, between an individual and its properties. Consider the redness of this book. On Spinoza's theory this is a mode of God. Why then should we ascribe the redness to the *book* and not to God,

59

and why do we feel such reluctance to see the book as a *property* of God? How can a finite mode be conceived as an independent individual, and not just as a transient state of something else, in which it inheres?

Spinoza often refers to finite individuals, and speaks of this or that finite mode 'in so far as (*quatem* or *quatenus*) it is in itself' (for example *E* 3, 6). In other words, there is a sense in which—or a point to which—finite modes may be self-dependent ('in' themselves) in the way that God is self-dependent. Spinoza also provides a definition of essence (*E* 2, Definition 2) which may be applied as well to finite modes as to God:

> that pertains to the essence of a thing which, when granted, necessarily involves the granting of the thing, and which, when removed, necessarily involves the removal of the thing; or that without which the thing, or on the other hand, which without the thing can neither exist nor be conceived.

Spinoza's application of these ideas to finite modes involves an interesting inversion of Descartes' argument about the wax (see Chapter 3).

The wax seemed to possess no essential unity or identity beyond that of the stuff out of which it was composed. It could be broken up, melted down, transformed in respect of every one of its properties except those which pertain to matter (or extension) as such. It is tempting to conclude that only extension is preserved through every change. (The individuality of the piece of wax, we might say, is dissolved in its constitution.) By contrast, Spinoza observes, there are things which have a kind of inherent resistance to the changes undergone by the lump of wax. They resist damage, fracture or melting; sometimes, if injured, they restore themselves out of their own inherent principle of self-recovery. They endeavour, as Spinoza puts it, to persist in their own being. This endeavour (*conatus*) constitutes their essence, since it is that which, when removed, necessarily involves the removal of the thing, and that without which the thing cannot exist. Moreover, the *conatus* of a thing is the causal principle in terms of which we explain its persistence and its properties. The more *conatus* it has, therefore, the more an object is self-dependent—the more it is 'in itself'.

The obvious examples are organisms. Consider animals: unlike stones they avoid injury, resist it when it is threatened, and even restore themselves when it is inflicted —unless the injury is so serious as to destroy *conatus* altogether. For this reason we attribute to animals a self-dependence and an individuality that we rarely accord to inanimate things. This is borne out by our ways of describing them, using always 'count nouns' rather than 'mass nouns'. A stone is a *lump* of stone, a lake is a *pool* of water, a snowman is a *heap* of snow. But until dead a cat is an individual cat and not a lump of cat: only when the *conatus* has expired could it be described as a heap, a lump, or a mass. The individuality and self-dependence of a cat, like those of a man, are part of its *nature*, and to divide a cat in two is to create, not two half-pieces of cat, but two whole pieces of something else. The cat endeavours to persist as *one* thing, and exists just so long as that endeavour is, in Spinoza's mathematical idiom, 'granted'.

The endeavour of the body is also an endeavour of the mind. Conceived in mental terms, this endeavour is what we mean by will (*voluntas*). Sometimes we refer to both body and mind in describing a creature's *conatus*, and then we speak of 'appetite'; sometimes—especially when describing people—we wish to emphasize the element of consciousness that leads them not only to have appetites but also to be aware of them: then we use the term 'desire' (*cupiditas*) (*E* 3, 9). In every case, however, we are referring to the same reality: the *conatus* that causes an organism to stand apart from its surroundings, in a persistent and active self-dependence.

The theory of *conatus*, combined with Spinoza's analysis of the relation between body and mind, has a peculiar consequence, namely, that 'the mind . . . endeavours to persist in its being for an indefinite period, and is conscious of this its endeavour' (*E* 3, 9). Hence it is impossible to contemplate suicide: (in Spinoza's words: 'the idea which cuts off the existence of our body cannot be given in our mind, but is contrary thereto' (*E* 3, 10)). Intentional suicide is a contradiction, since it involves a deliberate striving not to strive, a self-generated violation of one's own self-generation, a pitting of one's essence against itself. How then does Spinoza explain the many cases of actual suicide? And how does he reconcile his theory with his own ethics, which tells us not to fear death, and not to shun death for ignoble reasons (*E* 4, 72; *E* 5, 38)?

Spinoza's official answer to this difficulty is that 'nothing can be destroyed save by an external cause' (*E* 3, 4), and hence that 'no one . . . kills himself from the necessity of his own nature. Those who do such things are compelled by external causes, which can happen in many ways' (*E* 4, 20, Scholium). He gives various examples, citing the case of Seneca, who opened his veins at the command of a tyrant, and that of madness, in which the mind has 'assumed a nature contrary to its former one'. This new nature is one of which an idea could not be given in the mind so long as the mind conformed to its original endeavour; hence it is not the outcome of the mind's *conatus*.

Commentators express varying degrees of dissatisfaction

with Spinoza's theory of suicide. What is important, however, is to see that he does in fact present a theory, and that it is not without penetration. It is wholly characteristic of Spinoza to follow through the consequences of his own metaphysics, to these points of contact with the human world. Had he remained dreaming in abstract spheres, unconscious of, or reluctant to face, the real problems of human life and understanding, his system would be of far less interest than it is. In this particular case, he overlooked many possible explanations of suicide. But it is not obvious that he is wrong in his fundamental postulate, that all things seriously undertaken by *me*, are undertaken for the sake of my persistence. The noble suicides of Japan show clearly enough, how a man can desire to end himself, precisely so as to persist in his ending.

The theory of ideas

Everything can be conceived either as idea or as extended thing; and yet there is no causal relation (in any sense recognizable by Spinoza) between mind and body. A causal relation exists between two things only if the conception of one involves the conception of the other. An idea may depend upon another idea for its conception, and a body likewise on another body. But at no point in the elaboration of the system of ideas can intelligible reference be made to a physical mode, nor, in the elaboration of the science of extension, can intelligible reference be made to the mental. The two systems are parallel but incommensurable expressions of a single totality. Nevertheless, 'the order and connection of ideas is the same as the order and connection of things' (*E* 2, 7). Hence there is no difficulty in relating the mind to things outside it, or in displaying its position in the unfolding sequence of *natura naturata*:

The order or concatenation of things is one, whether nature is conceived under one or the other attribute; it follows therefore that the order of the actions and passions of our body is simultaneous with the order of the actions and passions of the mind . . . (thus) the decision of the mind, together with the appetite and determination of the body, are simultaneous in nature, or rather that they are one and the same thing, which, when it is considered under the attribute of thought and explained in terms of it, we call decision, and when considered under the attribute of extension, and deduced from the laws of motion and rest, we call causation.

(*E* 3, 2, Scholium)

And for every idea there is an *ideatum*—an object conceived under the attribute of extension, which exactly corresponds to the idea in the system of the world. Every idea is 'of' its *ideatum*, and every idea therefore displays what Spinoza called the 'extrinsic' mark of truth, namely an exact and necessary correspondence to its *ideatum* (*E* 2, Definition 4). This does not imply that there is no such thing as a false idea. For many ideas fail to possess the 'intrinsic' marks of truth. Error stems from our failure to grasp the full system of ideas, and the relations of dependence which hold between them; hence we remain with confused or partial conceptions of things, and only by replacing these conceptions with 'adequate' ideas can we have any guarantee that our thought displays things as they are. Only in the 'adequate' idea are the intrinsic marks of truth discernible (*E* 2, Definition 4). Spinoza's 'adequate' is meant to perform a similar function to Descartes' 'clear and distinct'; indeed, Spinoza sometimes uses the Cartesian terminology (for example at *E* 2, 28, in *S*, *M*, and in early letters). However, the theory of the 'adequate' idea is far more systematic than its Cartesian prototype, and leads to conclusions which Descartes would certainly have rejected.

An idea which possesses only the extrinsic mark of truth may be a source of error—and in this sense may be described as false. While we can know that it corresponds (as it must) to its *ideatum*, we cannot know, from the intrinsic properties of the idea, just what that *ideatum* is. The inadequate idea, in other words, is opaque to the world, while the adequate idea is transparent. Hence 'between a true and an adequate idea I recognise no difference, except that the epithet "true" only has regard to the agreement between the idea and its ideatum, whereas the epithet "adequate" has regard to the nature of the idea itself' (*C* LX).

From the rationalist assumption that there really *are* adequate ideas, Spinoza shows how to construct a theory of knowledge (which is in fact a theory of error). The theory (roughly worked out in *S* 2, 15 and 16, and perfected in *E* 2, 35ff.) is exceedingly intricate, and rendered particularly difficult by Spinoza's constant tendency to describe the relation between idea and *ideatum* as one of representation (so that an idea sometimes seems to be *of* its *ideatum*, in the normal understanding of that difficult word, and not simply in the sense implied by Spinoza's metaphysics). In medieval parlance, Spinoza constantly describes as an intentional relation (a relation in thought) what is in fact a material relation (a relation in fact). Spinoza was probably not confused on this point, although he might have been clearer. Thus he sometimes uses the word 'object' (*objectum*) to refer to the representational content of an idea, reserving the word '*ideatum*' for its correlate (for example *E* 2, 13, Scholium, and see the Glossary).

Like Descartes, Spinoza uses the term 'idea' to cover all

mental contents. He therefore crosses, in his use of the term, two critical frontiers: that between concept and perception, and that between concept and proposition. There is surely a distinction between the concept of man and a perception, image or dream of a man; and a distinction between the concept of man and the proposition that a man exists. For Spinoza, however, these distinctions have to be reconstructed from the intricate leavings of his epistemology—and Spinoza devotes some fascinating and brilliant pages to the task of reconstructing them (*E* 2, 16 and 17; *E* 2, 48 and 49). The student of Spinoza must therefore remember that, contained within the very proposition that a given idea is true, is an ambiguity so great as to make interpretation frequently almost impossible.

By explaining truth as an intrinsic property of adequate ideas, Spinoza closes the gap between the world and our adequate conception of it. He also offers a proof, interesting in detail, and imaginative in manner, that every adequate idea is self-evident to the person who possesses it (*E* 2, 43). His principal concern is therefore with the explanation, first of error, and secondly of the ordinary, imperfect knowledge whereby we conduct our lives.

'Falsity', Spinoza argues (*E* 2, 35), 'consists in privation of knowledge, resulting from inadequate or mutilated and confused ideas'. A prime example of inadequacy is sensory perception. Consider the sun, as it appears to a man studying it from the earth. The image which constitutes the perception of the sun is indeed an idea. But the *ideatum* of that idea is not what the perceiver takes it to be. It is not the sun, which is represented quite falsely as a small red ball a few feet in diameter swimming through a sea of blue. The true *ideatum* of this idea is, rather, the modification in the body of which it is, so to speak, the mental aspect. (The *ideatum* is, as we should now say, a process in the nervous system.) Being inadequate, however, the idea is referred not to the bodily process which is its material correlate, but to the sun, of which it presents only confused and partial cognition.

All knowledge gained through sense-perception is of that kind, and is assigned in the *Ethics* to the lowest of three levels of cognition. (There were four such levels in the *Treatise on the Emendation of the Intellect* and again three in the *Short Treatise*; the inspiration is in both cases classical, Aristotle having argued for four levels of cognition, Plato for three.) Spinoza calls this first level of cognition imagination or opinion, and implies that such cognition can never reach adequacy, since the ideas of imagination come to us, not in their intrinsic logical order, but in the order of our bodily processes. The ideas of imagination are the illogical reflections of processes that are inadequately comprehended. By the steady accumulation of confused ideas we can arrive at an apprehension of what is common to them—a universal notion (*notio universalis*)—such as is exemplified in our common conceptions of man, tree, dog or warthog-minder (*E* 2, 40, Scholium). One reason for distrusting ordinary language as a philosophical instrument is that the ideas conveyed by it belong, on the whole, to this class of composite but confused conceptions, and not to the class of adequate ideas.

To return to the example: the sun cannot be adequately known through modifications of our body, but only through the science which aims to provide an adequate idea of the sun. This kind of science, proceeding by reasoned reflection from first principles, exemplifies Spinoza's second level of cognition, involving adequate ideas and 'common notions' (*notiones communes*, to be distinguished from the 'universal notions' just referred to).

A common notion is an idea of some property which is common to everything, and 'those things which are common to all and which are equally in a part and in the whole, can only be conceived adequately' (*E* 2, 39). These notions are common too in another sense—namely that all men possess them, since all men partake of the common nature which they express. Such ideas, therefore, form the basic premises of natural science and provide the full and final explanation of the publicity of human knowledge and the possibility of philosophical communication.

Spinoza also recognizes a third level of knowledge, which he calls intuition or *scientia intuitiva*. 'This kind of cognition,' he explains, 'proceeds from an adequate idea of the formal essence of certain attributes of God to the adequate knowledge of the essence of things' (*E* 2, 40, Scholium 2). He illustrates that obscure remark with a mathematical example (expanded more fully in *S* II, Ch. 1), from which we may infer that, by 'intuition', Spinoza means the comprehensive grasp of the meaning and truth of a proposition which is vouchsafed to the person who grasps it together with a valid proof of it from self-evident premises, in a single mental act. Intuition had already been made central to epistemology by Descartes; Spinoza perfected Descartes' account, by describing intuition as an ideal of rational knowledge: a conception that is inextricably joined to its own valid proof. An intuition comes to us, according to Spinoza, only when we grasp the relation between the subject of study and an 'adequate idea of the formal essence of God', for nothing else can serve as the premise of a self-validating deduction. By 'formal essence' Spinoza means the real and independent nature of God. (The formal is distinguished from the 'objective': from the representation of something as an 'object' of thought, rather than as it is in itself (see *I* vi, 34–5). These scholastic terms provoke considerable confusion, since we should now use 'subjective' in place of 'objective' and 'real' in place of 'formal': see Glossary.)

Spinoza's theory of truth and cognition can now be briefly stated. 'Cognition of the first kind', he argues, 'is the only cause of falsity', whereas 'cognition of the second and third kinds is necessarily true' (*E* 2, 41). From our point of view, therefore, the truth of an idea is given in its logical connectedness to the system of 'adequate' ideas, and not merely in its extrinsic correspondence with its *ideatum*. The advancement of knowledge consists in the steady replacement of our confused and inadequate ideas with adequate conceptions, until, at the limit of apprehension, all that we think follows inexorably from an adequate idea of the essence of God.

'Sub specie aeternitatis'

All ideas exist in God, as modifications of his thinking. Some ideas also exist in the human mind. Spinoza therefore says that our ideas exist in God *in so far as* (*quatenus*) he constitutes the human mind. Conversely, since God has adequate knowledge of everything, our own ideas are adequate *in so far as* we share in the infinite intellect. Spinoza assumes that this 'in so far as' is a matter of degree: the more adequate my conceptions, the more I reach beyond my finite condition to the divine essence of which I am a mode.

It is not easy to understand the idiom 'in so far as'. Nevertheless, without this idiom, the most important of the links in Spinoza's argument—the link between the divine and the human—is destroyed. As I argued in the last chapter, it is only in a manner of speaking that we can describe God's attributes in temporal terms. God is eternal, which means that he is outside time and change. Hence:

'things are conceived as actual in two ways—either in so far as they exist in relation to a certain time and place, or in so far as we conceive them as contained in God, and following from the necessity of the divine nature' (*E* 5, 29, Scholium). To pass from the divine to the human is to pass from the timeless to time. Although the modifications of God are understood by us as 'enduring' and as succeeding each other in time, this permeation of our knowledge by the concept of time reflects only the inadequacy of our cognition. 'In so far as' we perceive things adequately we understand them as flowing from God's eternal nature, by a chain of explanation which is logical, and therefore atemporal, in form.

Thus, in Spinoza's words, 'it is the nature of reason to perceive things under a certain aspect of eternity (*sub quadam aeternitatis specie*)' (*E* 2, 44, Corollary 2). An adequate conception of the world is a conception *sub specie aeternitatis*; that is how God sees the world (with which he is identical), and that is how we see it, *in so far as* our minds participate in the vision which is God's.

Spinoza attempts to prove, and the *Ethics* is supposed to exemplify, that 'the human mind has an adequate knowledge of the eternal and infinite essence of God' (*E* 2, 47). (What is proved here, however, was also assumed at the outset.) By achieving adequate knowledge we come to understand what is divine and eternal. On the other hand, we understand our own nature and identity *sub specie durationis*—under the aspect of time. For it is as enduring and finite modes that we enjoy the *conatus* that distinguishes us from the self-sufficient whole of things, and to know *ourselves* as separate, individual existences, is to be locked in the time-bound conception that leads to confused and partial knowledge. Man's condition is essentially one of conflict: reason aspires towards the eternal totality, while the concerns of sensuous existence persist only so long as we see things temporally and partially. The message of Spinoza's ethics can be succinctly put: our salvation consists in seeing the world *sub specie aeternitatis*, and in gaining, thereby, freedom from the bondage of time.

So long as we remain locked in the concerns that flow from our perishable identity, we imagine ourselves to be free. But 'men are mistaken in thinking themselves free, and this opinion consists in this alone, that they are conscious of their actions and ignorant of the causes whereby they are determined' (*E* 2, 35, Scholium). The idea of liberty, then, is an error of imagination and provides neither guidance nor happiness to the man who is enslaved by it. Reason, unlike imagination, sees things not as contingent but as necessary (*E* 2, 44). The more we understand, therefore, the more we are convinced of the unreality of temporal freedom, and the more do we see the truth calmly enunciated in *E* 2, 48, that 'there is in no mind absolute or free will, but the mind is determined to will this or that by a cause which is determined by another cause, and this one again by another, and so on ad infinitum'. Such infinite chains of causal necessity are simply the reflection, *sub specie durationis*, of that which, seen *sub specie aeternitatis*, is the eternal and immutable will of God.

The illusion that we can be free *in* time gives way to the certainty that we can be free *from* time. It is this real and higher freedom that Spinoza goes on to recommend.

5 Freedom

Something is missing from Spinoza's philosophy of mind: something decisive, whose presence or absence affects the whole character of a philosopher's thinking. This missing element is the self, or subject: the focal point of Descartes' reasoning, whose existence was established by the *cogito*. True, Spinoza adopts as an axiom in Part 2 of the *Ethics* that 'man thinks', and there is, in *E* 2, 11, an obscure echo of the Cartesian argument: 'the first thing which constitutes the actual being of the human mind is nothing else than the idea of an individual thing actually existing.' But in neither of those propositions does one find the 'I' which, for Descartes, was the necessary bastion against hyperbolical doubt. Indeed, Spinoza makes clear in the preface to the *Principles of Cartesian Philosophy* that he recognizes no special authority in the *cogito*, beyond the authority of 'clear and distinct ideas', and these represent the world not from the point of view of the subject, but *sub specie aeternitatis*: in other words, from the 'point of view' of God.

Spinoza *does* recognize the existence of self-conscious-ness, which he characterizes roughly thus: our ideas may be accompanied by ideas of themselves, and those ideas by ideas of *them*, and so on ad infinitum. Spinoza tries to explain this by proving that 'the idea of the mind is united to the mind in the same manner as the mind is united to the body' (*E* 2, 21). The proof is, however, one of the least clear and least persuasive of his arguments, largely because it makes no mention of the crucial concept that is in issue: the concept of the self. True to the method of adequate ideas, Spinoza can find no way to insert, into the heart of his universe, the subjective viewpoint from which it is surveyed.

Ethics and the absolute view

The task of philosophy, as Descartes conceived it, was to ascend from the point of view of the subject to the 'absolute conception' of the world (as Bernard Williams has described it), i.e. to the conception of the world from no point of view within it. Knowledge consists in the elimination of the subject from the description of what is known. In the *Critique of Pure Reason*, Kant was to argue decisively that this purging of all reference to the subject is neither possible nor desirable: the world is *my* world, stamped indelibly with the mark of self-awareness. For Spinoza, however, the assumption of the absolute conception is fundamental; for this is precisely what 'adequate' knowledge consists in.

The consequences for moral philosophy are considerable. Spinoza sees life from the point of view, not of an 'I' whose problems arise from his individual circumstances, but of a pure and disinterested reasoner, for whom the human individual is nothing but a mode of God, governed by the laws which govern everything. It is precisely in this objective, 'selfless' view of the world that Spinoza finds the basis of his moral counsels, arguing that we should rise above the illusory perspective which sees things *sub specie durationis*, to that absolute viewpoint which is God's. Only then, he believes, will we be truly free, and only in that intellectual freedom are we fulfilled.

Good and evil

In our ordinary lives, when seeing the world *sub specie durationis*, we see also a great divide between good and evil, and are torn between the demands of morality and the temptations of nature. Those attitudes, however, derive from the first level of cognition; an adequate idea of our nature eliminates the conflict between reason and passion, which is no more than a product of our confused opinions.

73

Spinoza gave what would now be called an 'emotivist' theory of moral judgement. The use of words like 'good' and 'bad' is to be explained, not by the truth of the ideas expressed in them, but by the emotions which they are used to convey: 'we do not strive towards, desire or long for nothing because we deem it to be good; but on the contrary, we deem a thing good because we strive, wish, desire or long for it' (*E* 3, 9). And elsewhere, in the preface to Part 4 of the *Ethics*, in *S* 51, 60 and in various letters, Spinoza elaborates this idea, arguing that moral and aesthetic judgements are alike relative to the attitudes and interests of the subject, and contain only the most confused apprehension of the nature of things. Each person's use of such terms as 'good' and 'bad' will be governed by his own particular desires and ambitions, and nothing could be learned about the world from the ideas expressed in our moral judgements.

Spinoza goes further, arguing, in language reminiscent of Maimonides, that 'it is only in speaking improperly, or humanly, that we say that we sin against God' (*C* XIX). In his answer to the 'problem of evil' (the problem of reconciling an evil world with a good creator), Spinoza adopts the solution of Maimonides (*Guide to the Perplexed*, iii, 21), and argues that the things which seem to us to be evils are merely 'privations'—that is, partial or truncated modes of God, which 'express no essence' (*C* XXIII, *E* 4, Preface): to the extent that they are evil, to that extent are they also unreal.

The combination of emotivism and the Maimonidean solution to the problem of evil might seem to bring the work of the moral philosopher to an end. If the ideas of good and evil are arbitrary and subjective, and if everything that happens is alike part of the divine perfection, what objective moral advice can be offered? In fact Spinoza believes that much can be said. Like Aristotle—his un-acknowledged master throughout Parts 3 and 4 of the *Ethics*—he believes that moral questions can be objectively posed and objectively answered. Once we see through the veil of the passions and understand human nature as it really is, we perceive that our freedom and our happiness are one and the same, and that the good life for man is both objectively definable, and rationally pursuable. The 'good life' is not defined by this or that person's moral judgements, but objectively, by human nature. Hence Spinoza offers his own technical definitions of the words 'good' and 'bad', in terms of which to conduct a 'geometrical' investigation into human happiness: 'by good, I understand that which we certainly know to be useful (*utile*) to us'; 'by bad, however, I understand that which we certainly know will prevent us from partaking of any good' (*E* 4, Definitions 1 and 2). The good life is that which is most 'useful'— favourable—to our nature; the bad life that which is most opposed to it. Vice and wickedness are to be avoided, not because they are punished by God (who engages in no such absurd endeavours), but because they are at variance with our nature, and lead us to despair (*C* XXI).

Active and passive

In Proposition 1 of Part 3 of the *Ethics* a distinction is made between 'active' and 'passive' states of mind: 'Our mind acts certain things and suffers others: namely in so far as it has adequate ideas, thus far it necessarily acts certain things, and in so far as it has inadequate ideas, thus far it necessarily suffers certain things.' The distinction between doing things and suffering things is a distinction of degree, and, since only God is the full and originating cause of anything, only he acts without being acted upon. Finite modes, such as we are, constitute links in the infinite chains of causality which bind the world. Nevertheless, 'in so far as' our states are generated from within—from the *conatus* or striving that constitutes our nature—so far are we the cause of them, and so far are we active in respect of them. Conversely, in so far as we are acted upon by external causes, so far are we passive: the victims of processes which we do not control.

It is precisely by possessing adequate ideas that we advance from the passive to the active state. Spinoza proves this by an ingenious play on the word *quatenus* ('in so far as'). In *E* 2, 11, Corollary, he had proved that 'ideas which are adequate in the mind of anyone are adequate in God in so far as he constitutes the essence of that mind'. Now from any given idea some effect must follow, and an adequate idea is the adequate cause (i.e. full explanation) of all that flows from it. Hence God, who has adequate ideas, is the full or adequate cause of things. And 'in so far as he is affected by an idea which is adequate in the mind of someone, that same mind is the adequate cause of', and hence 'necessarily acts' certain things.

Spinoza's conception of mental activity corresponds only distantly to our ordinary conceptions of will and agency. However, it is useful to consider an example. Suppose that a gust of wind throws me against my companion, and he falls. In this transaction I am passive, receiving the force of the wind and passing it mechanically to my neighbour. Such ideas as I have of the process are confused and inadequate perceptions arising from the bodily processes which afflict me. Suppose now that I conceive a plan to assault my companion, and choosing the moment, strike him down. Here I am (in normal parlance) active in producing the same effect. A process of reasoning preceded it which, while it did not necessitate the outcome, represented more accurately than my confused perception of the wind's pressure, the process which led to my neighbour's fall. Spinoza would perhaps say that this reasoning is a 'more adequate' idea of the process leading to action, hence a fuller explanation, hence a completer cause.

If it were possible for me to have a *wholly* adequate idea of the process, then I should be *wholly* active in relation to it. As it is, I am active only *in so far as* my ideas are adequate, and of something so finite and limited as a falling body I can have no adequate conception. Hence my striking my companion, while more of an action than my falling against him, was still very much a passion. Moreover, for Spinoza, we may be completely active in respect of processes which are in no ordinary sense actions of our own: for example, a man falling through space, granted an adequate conception of what is happening to him, is active; while one deliberately striking his companion, but ignorant of the universal laws of motion, is passive. With complete actions we have little acquaintance, save in the realm of mathematical and philosophical reasoning, where one idea follows from another with a necessity that is wholly self-evident to us. And in obeying this necessity, Spinoza goes on to argue, we are completely free.

Such considerations may help us to understand Spinoza's strange doctrine, that 'the actions of the mind arise from adequate ideas alone, while passions depend upon inadequate ideas alone' (*E* 3, 3), although the doctrine can perhaps be fully understood only in terms of the concealed assumption that I identified in Chapter 3, section 2 (which holds that the order of the world is the order of adequate ideas). The mind is active, for Spinoza, in so far as it is self-determining, freed from the influence of things of which it has no adequate idea.

Adequacy of ideas is tantamount to power; the more my ideas are adequate, the more am I independent. This

independence from the world is what Spinoza calls virtue;
and 'by virtue (*virtus*) and power I understand the same
thing' (*E* 4, Definition 8). Virtue is also perfection, and for
Spinoza perfection and reality are one and the same. In the
case of a human being, therefore, virtue consists in the
enhancement of the *conatus* through which he persists.
Finally, 'pleasure' (*laetitia*) is defined as 'the passion with
which the mind passes to a higher state of perfection', and
'pain' (*tristitia*) as 'the passion by which it passes to a lower
state of perfection' (*E* 3, 11). By a combination of
outrageous metaphysics and brazen definitions, therefore,
Spinoza arrives promptly at the conclusion of his moral
philosophy: that it is in our nature constantly to increase
our power, that this is the source of all pleasure, and that
the process whereby we obtain this pleasure is the very
same 'improvement of the intellect' that leads us to
adequate ideas. If there were nothing more to Spinoza's
argument than that, we should rightly set it aside as
sophistry and self-deception. But we must remember, first,
that the metaphysics lends itself to many interpretations,
and secondly that Spinoza's definitions are intended, not
as a substitute for argument, but as the first moves in an
argument which reveals more exactly what he means.

The geometry of the passions

Spinoza founds his moral philosophy in a 'natural history'
of man: but it is a special kind of natural history, derived
entirely deductively, from premises deemed to be necessarily true. He remarks on the originality of such an attempt:

> Most of those who have written about the passions, and
> men's way of living, seem to treat, not of natural things,
> which follow the common laws of nature, but of things
> which are outside nature. Indeed they seem to conceive
> man in nature as a dominion within a dominion. . . . To

them it will doubtless seem most strange . . . that I should attempt to treat of the vices and failings of man in a geometrical manner, and should wish to demonstrate with accurate reasoning those things which they cry out against as opposed to reason, as vain, absurd, and disgusting . . . [However] such emotions as hate, wrath, envy, etc., considered in themselves, follow from the same necessity and ability of nature as other individual things: and therefore they acknowledge certain causes through which they are understood, and have certain properties equally worthy of our knowledge as the properties of any other thing . . .   (*E* 3, Preface)

It follows from the truth of Spinoza's metaphysics, then, that a geometry of the passions is possible, and that no other study of them will lead us to self-knowledge. Spinoza therefore proposes to treat of the emotions (*affectiones*) exactly as he had treated of God, regarding 'human actions and desires precisely as though I were dealing with lines, planes and bodies' (*E* 3, Preface).

The idea of a philosophical exposition of the human passions was by no means new. In the *Summa Theologica* Aquinas had presented an impressive survey of the subject in a style that is often close to Spinoza's, and with conclusions that display some of Spinoza's robust contempt for human self-deception. Descartes too had written a treatise on emotion, and in the *Leviathan* Hobbes had defined passions and motives in terms which clearly influenced Spinoza. In range and penetration, however, Spinoza far surpassed his immediate predecessors, and it is precisely in its application to this fraught and disturbing area that the merits of Spinoza's metaphysical detachment are most clearly displayed. Although he attempts, like Hobbes, to define the emotions in terms of a few simple ingredients (in his case, desire, pleasure and pain, together with their accompanying ideas and causal history), the ingredients in question are entities in a complex theory, by no means to be confused with the states of mind that we commonly call by the same names. Through his definitions, therefore, Spinoza provides a derivation from first principles of the fundamental properties of our feelings and the interconnections among them. There are many philosophers who would agree with Spinoza, for example, that we cannot hate a thing that we pity, or that no one envies the virtue of anyone save his equal; and who would agree with him too in seeing these propositions as necessary truths, to be established not by empirical investigation but by philosophical argument. But there are few philosophers who have provided such an illuminating network of necessary truths or such a striking answer to the question raised by them—the question, as Spinoza expresses it, of human servitude.

Spinoza describes love as pleasure accompanied by the idea of an external cause, and hate as pain similarly accompanied. He introduces these descriptions not as initial definitions, so much as résumés of interesting results, which want a name whereby they might be recorded. Only at the end of Part 3 does he lay out his definitions systematically, assuming that by then he has established that these definitions are not arbitrary ploys of nomenclature, but approximations to the 'real essence' of the things described. By then Spinoza has also established such propositions as the following: that 'if we imagine anything to affect with pleasure what we love, we are affected with love towards it' (*E* 3, 22); that we 'imitate' the emotions of those things which we imagine to be like ourselves (*E* 3, 27); that our loves and hatred are reinforced by the imagination that others share in them (*E* 3, 32); that we endeavour to bring it about that our love is reciprocated

(*E* 3, 33); that we hate those who are our rivals in love, and are affected by sexual jealousy with obscene thoughts (*E* 3, 35, especially Scholium); and so on. All such truths are, for Spinoza, necessary truths about the essence of man, founded not on observation but on rational deduction from two opaque and abstract axioms concerning the 'affections' of the human body.

The Amendment of the Passions

Spinoza defines emotion (*affectus*—see Glossary) in general terms thus:

> Emotion, which is called passivity of the soul (*pathema animi*) is a confused idea wherewith the mind affirms a greater or less power of existing (*vis existendi*) of its body or of any part of it than before, and which, being granted, the mind is thereby determined to think one thing rather than another.   (*E* 3, Appendix)

In this definition he conveys two fundamental truths about emotion: first, its connection with our existence as embodied creatures, propelled by forces which we do not wholly understand; secondly, its character as a 'mental affirmation' or judgement. An emotion, in other words, is a *form* of understanding, however confused, in which a greater or less 'activity' of the mind might be expressed. Spinoza, explaining his definition—which like all his definitions in this part is offered as a conclusion and not a premise of the argument—argues thus:

> inasmuch as the essence of the mind consists in this (2, 11 and 13), that it affirms the actual existence of its body, and as we understand by perfection the very essence of the thing, it follows, therefore, that the mind passes to a greater or less perfection when it happens to affirm something confirming its body, or some part of it, which involves more or less reality than before. (*E* 3, Appendix)

Thus the 'mental act' which lies at the heart of every

passion may express a greater or less mental perfection, a greater or less reality, a greater or less power. As the metaphysics implies, perfection, reality and power are one and the same, and in their mental aspect they are equivalent to the 'adequacy' of ideas. Emotions, therefore, are ranged on a scale, according to the 'adequacy' of the idea involved in them; from the extreme of passion, in which the mind is the helpless victim of processes which it does not grasp, to the extreme of mental action, in which, through serene contemplation of the truth of things, the mind asserts its perfection, and its power.

The 'emendation' of the passions consists precisely in the transition from passion to action, in which the intellect gains ascendancy over the disordered material of the imagination. Thus, 'an emotion which is a passion ceases to be a passion as soon as we form a clear and distinct idea of it' (*E* 5, 3), from which it follows, Spinoza argues, that 'the more an emotion becomes known to us, the more it is within our power, and the less the mind is passive to it' (*E* 5, 3, Corollary).

Several recent philosophers—notably Stuart Hampshire —have greeted this aspect of Spinoza's philosophy with acclaim, believing it to involve an early version of Freudian analysis: a metaphysical grounding to Freud's dictum that 'where there was *id* there shall be *ego*' (in Spinoza's terms: where I was enslaved by confused ideas, generated by processes of which I had no clear awareness, I shall be free, possessing only adequate ideas of my motives). Such philosophers praise Spinoza for recognizing the extent to which our emotional life is, in the natural course of things, hidden from us, and hidden precisely by its dependence upon our bodily history. And they further commend Spinoza for his recognition that we are not without weapons in our encounter with these unconscious forces: that, by an effort of self-understanding we may bring to the surface that which is at present concealed, and in doing so become active, decisive, and dominant over our own emotional condition. We cease to be victims, and instead become masters, of a fate which is nevertheless ours.

Spinoza's theory of the human agent certainly lends itself to the view that we are largely governed by 'unconscious' forces. As I have suggested, there is, for Spinoza, no 'self', no 'first person' who takes charge, so to speak, of the causality of my actions. Moreover, the cognition which is presented to me in so confused a form by my passions is a cognition of the *body*: for Spinoza, therefore, it can be amended only by a better cognition—an 'adequate idea'—of the natural processes which that body displays. Nevertheless, one could see in these ideas, not the strength of Spinoza's theory of emotion, but its weakness—in particular, its inability to account for the two most important features of our emotional life: the status of the self as subject of emotion, and of the world (the other) as object. Emotions are directed outwards: they focus, or 'intend', an object, and direct our energies towards that object. Spinoza's theory recognizes this fact (the fact of 'intentionality') but radically misdescribes it. For Spinoza the 'directedness' of an emotion—as we experience it—is no better than an illusion, a confused representation of processes which exist, not in the surrounding world, but in the body of the subject. (Cf. Spinoza's account of perception, considered earlier, pp.66–7.) I understand my love for you, therefore, not by understanding *you*, who are its object, nor by understanding *myself*, who am its subject, but by understanding this strange interloper, my body, in which love grows inscrutably like a cancer, erupting into consciousness in ways which inform me only dimly of the processes by which my mind is enslaved.

Against that picture one may reasonably affirm that an emotion is an attempt to understand, not the body, but the other person, and oneself in relation to him. The true emendation of the passions consists in a deepening understanding of the other, not as a physical object, but as a self like me. For Spinoza the other is at best a link in the chain of causes that leads to my idea of him, and in no sense the real matter (the *ideatum*) of my emotion. To see in such a view some deep truth about human emotion is to have forgotten what it is to be human. Spinoza can be forgiven, in that his theory of ideas—if accepted—restores, in reconstructed form, the basic contours of our human intentionality. But his Freudian disciples, who stop short of accepting the theory of the 'adequate idea', and who take Spinoza to be justifying the morbid morality of the psychoanalyst, are perhaps less blameless in their praise of him, than he himself in first inspiring it.

Freedom and power

Nietzsche too might have joined in praising a philosopher whom he dismissed as a 'sickly recluse', had he studied more patiently the argument that man's happiness and freedom consist in the constant increase of his power, and that not only hatred, envy, contempt and rage, but also pity and humility are weaknesses, which have no place in the life of a superior being (*E* 5, 50, 53). (Nietzsche notices the argument, but promptly discards it; see *The Genealogy of Morals*, 2, xv.) Spinoza's positive morality is striking as much for its defiance of the received ideas of Christian civilization, as for its 'geometrical' rigour, and even those who are unpersuaded by the 'selfless' metaphysics upon which it is founded, will profit from the wise attention to the human reality which informs its principal conclusions.

The positive morality has two sides, one worldly,

consisting in the disciplined emendation of the passions that I have just sketched—the other more religious, or at any rate contemplative, in tone. The first harks back to Aristotle, and Spinoza's proofs (*E* 4, 52) that 'self-complacency (*acquiescentia in se ipso*) is the highest object for which we can hope', and (*E* 4, 58) that 'honour (*gloria*) is not repugnant to reason but may arise from it', echo the pivotal thoughts of Aristotle's philosophy of virtue. The second side of Spinoza's philosophy is more Platonic in character, and recalls the great work of neo-Platonic morality which cheered countless medieval poets and divines along the path of Christian renunciation: the *Consolation of Philosophy* by Boethius. It is in this part of his moral theory that Spinoza confronts most directly the problem of human freedom.

According to Definition 7 of Part 1 'that thing is said to be free (*libera*) which exists by the mere necessity of its own nature and is determined in its actions by itself alone'. By this definition only God is free; human action, which stems necessarily from the divine nature (i.e. from an 'external cause') is therefore 'compelled' (ibid.). God's freedom is identical with his power: his power to produce his own modifications without reference to an external cause. It is possible, by means of the dubious locution 'in so far as' (*quatenus*), to extend the idea of freedom to finite modes. In so far as we are the 'adequate' causes of our own actions, thus far are we the producers of them without the aid of an external cause, and thus far, therefore, are we free. We approximate to this state of self-dependence to the extent that our mind is occupied with adequate ideas. The very same 'emendation of the passions', that leads us to an adequate conception of the world, leads us also to emancipation: to that power over our own situation which is all that we can genuinely mean by freedom.

Spinoza therefore introduces a subsidiary definition of freedom (*E* 4, 24): 'man can be called free only in so far as he has the power to exist and act in accordance with the laws of human nature', which means (*T* xvi, *P* ii, 11) 'to seek and find understanding'. Such a freedom in no way implies that human action is released from necessity. In particular, we must set aside the vulgar idea of freedom according to which human actions are free because contingent. The ideas of 'contingency' and 'possibility', Spinoza argues, signify not real features of the world, but only 'defects of our intellect' (*M* 1, iii, section 9; *E* 1, 33, Scholium 1); we can therefore define them in terms of a deficiency of knowledge:

> I call individual things contingent in so far as, while we regard their essence alone, we find nothing which imposes their existence necessarily, or which necessarily excludes it. I call the same individual things possible in so far as while we regard the causes by which they must be produced, we know not whether they are determined to produce them. (*E* 4, Definitions 3 and 4)

The common idea of human freedom, which belongs to the first level of cognition, is one that enshrines our ignorance:

> Further conceive, I beg, that a stone, while continuing in motion, should be capable of thinking and knowing, that it is endeavouring, as far as it can, to continue to move. Such a stone, being conscious merely of its own endeavour and not at all indifferent, would believe itself to be completely free, and would think that it continued in motion solely because of its own wish. This is that human freedom, which all boast that they possess, and which consists solely in the fact that men are conscious of their own desire, but are ignorant of the causes whereby that desire has been determined. (*C* LVIII)

The more we know of the causality of our actions, the less room do we have for ideas of possibility and contingency. However, the knowledge of causality does not cancel the belief in freedom, but vindicates it. It is the *illusory* idea of freedom, arising from imagination, that creates our bondage; for we believe in the contingency of things only in so far as our mind is passive. The more we see things as necessary (through the medium of adequate ideas) the more do we increase our power over them, and so the more are we free (*E* 5, 6). Freedom is not freedom from necessity, but rather the consciousness of necessity. In a mathematical proof our mind is wholly determined by logical necessity, and at the same time wholly 'in control': and this, for Spinoza, is our paradigm of freedom. If freedom were freedom from the necessities of logic it could be of no value (*C* XXI).

The free man is the man conscious of the necessities that compel him. Spinoza devotes many pages to describing the mental condition of such a man. He avoids hatred, envy, contempt and other negative emotions; he is unaffected by fear, hope and superstition; he is secure in the knowledge that virtue is power, power is freedom, and freedom is happiness. 'A free man thinks of nothing less than of death, and his wisdom is a meditation not on death but on life' (*E* 4, 17). His blessedness consists in the serene contemplation of the whole of things, bound in community with like-minded spirits, by 'the love which acknowledges as its cause freedom of mind' (*E* 4, Appendix).

Moreover 'he who understands himself and his emotions loves God, and the more so the more he understands himself and his emotions' (*E* 5, 15). This love, which stems necessarily from the pursuit of knowledge, is an intellectual love (*amor intellectualis Dei*). The mind is wholly active in loving God, and hence rejoices constantly, but passionlessly, in the object of its contemplation. God can experience neither passion, nor pleasure, nor pain (*E* 5, 17), and is therefore free from emotion. He neither loves the good not hates the wicked (*C* XXIII): indeed he loves and hates no one (*E* 5, 17, Corollary). Hence 'he who loves God cannot endeavour to bring it about that God should love him in return' (*E* 5, 19). Love towards God is wholly disinterested, and 'cannot be polluted by an emotion either of envy or jealousy, but is cherished the more, the more we imagine men to be bound to God by this bond of love' (*E* 5, 20). Indeed, man's intellectual love of God 'is the very love of God with which God loves himself' (*E* 5, 36). In loving God we participate more fully in the divine intellect, and in the impersonal, universal love that reigns there: for although God does not reciprocate our love, he nevertheless loves men, in so far as he loves himself in and through men. This eternal love constitutes our 'salvation, blessedness or liberty'.

Spinoza includes in his discussion of man's blessedness a singular and somewhat Platonistic proof of man's immortality—or rather, of the less satisfactory proposition that 'the human mind cannot be absolutely destroyed with the human body, but something of it remains which is eternal' (*E* 5, 23). The obscure proof of this proposition depends upon Spinoza's view that, through adequate ideas, the mind comes to see the world *sub specie aeternitatis*—in other words, without reference to time. The essence of the mind consists in the capacity for adequate ideas. The instantiation of this essence in time cannot be explained by adequate ideas, however, since they contain no temporal reference. Such ideas are given 'duration' only through their attachment to the mortal body, and not intrinsically:

Our mind therefore can be said to last, and its existence can be defined by a certain time, only in so far as it involves the actual existence of the body, and thus far only does it have the power to determine the existence of things by time, and to conceive them under the aspect of duration.   (*E* 5, 23, Scholium)

Some difficulties

Few commentators have found that proof (an earlier version of which occurs in *S*, II, 23) either convincing or wholly intelligible; for one thing, it seems to reject Spinoza's official theory of our embodiment. Nevertheless it is not without interest, in returning us to one of the fundamental problems of the system: the problem of time. Samuel Alexander argued that Spinoza, in common with many metaphysicians, 'failed to take time seriously': like Plato, Leibniz, and many other rationalists, Spinoza considered time to be, in some ultimate sense, unreal. '*Duration*' he argues (*C* XII), 'is only applicable to the existence of modes; *eternity* is applicable to the existence of substances'. Spinoza goes on to argue, in ways that bear a striking resemblance to the arguments of Kant, that 'measure, time and number are merely modes of thinking, or rather imagining' (*C*, ibid.). When understanding the world through the senses, we see it as ordered in time, and diversified in space. We therefore apply to it temporal and arithmetical notions, which have no application to the underlying reality. The universe of reason is timeless, and all that is true of it is true eternally.

How then can a rational being exist *in* time, so as to possess a life with which he is identified? Spinoza may have agreed with Eliot, that 'the point of intersection of the timeless with time/Is an occupation for the saint'; but to reach that point is already to pass beyond it, into a world that is wholly free from duration and its constraints. In that world there is neither motion nor passion nor diversity, but an eternal immutable calm. Hence:

> the wise man, in so far as he is considered as such, is
> scarcely moved in spirit: but, being conscious of himself,
> of God, and of things, by a certain eternal necessity, he
> never ceases to be, but possesses eternally true
> complacency (*acquiescentia*) of spirit.
>
> (*E* 5, 47, Scholium)

It would be fitting to leave Spinoza's ethics on that remark,
with which he himself brings it to its conclusion. But the
reader will have noticed once again the suspicious thread
which—were we to pull at it—might bring this noble
edifice to ruin. At the heart of Spinoza's thought, lies the
little word '*quatenus*', which seems to take away
everything that the philosopher proves, precisely by its
over-willing help in proving it. By means of this word
Spinoza repeatedly describes differences that are absolute
and impassable (those between God and man, eternity and
time, freedom and compulsion, action and passion,
independence and dependence) as differences of degree, so
suggesting a transition where no transition is possible.

Perhaps the most disturbing of all Spinoza's uses is in
referring to man 'in so far as' his ideas are adequate. By this
means he sometimes seems to suggest that we may have
more or less adequate conceptions of one and the same
thing, and therefore that adequacy too is a matter of degree.
Such a suggestion is strictly comparable to the view that a
proof might be more or less valid. The path that takes us to
the wisdom and blessedness of Spinoza involves many such
slides on the muddy *quatenus*. One of the pleasures in
following his political philosophy is that we can leave the
path to higher regions, and move more firmly and
comfortably downhill.

6 The body politic

The *Ethics* describes the free man, who has risen to the higher levels of cognition, mastered his passions and reached understanding of himself and the world. The populace, however, do not live as free men. They are led by imagination, and remain ignorant of the blessedness that comes through knowledge. At the same time men live in society, and the power of each of them is increased by their association. Even the free man—indeed, especially the free man—is drawn by love and honour to seek the company of those whose thoughts and feelings may profitably be joined to his own. It is therefore necessary to establish rules and principles whereby men might live in harmony, and for their common benefit. The problem requires a scientific answer: politics therefore becomes a philosophical concern.

Background
From the experience of civil war—first in the Netherlands, and then later, during Spinoza's lifetime, in England— came the two decisive works of post-Renaissance political thinking: *On the Law of War and Peace*, by Grotius, and the *Leviathan* by Hobbes. It is no small praise of Spinoza to say that his political writings bear comparison with those two masterpieces, and also with the *Prince* and the *Discourses* of Machiavelli, to which he was indebted for the style and structure of his *Political Treatise*.

There were few places in seventeenth-century Europe where a dissident Spanish Jew, who refused all compromise with the surrounding order, might live in peace. But the peace of the Netherlands had been bought at a price, and many of the conflicts and tensions that had exploded from time to time since the Union of Utrecht remained unresolved. The Netherlands of the seventeenth century bore no resemblance to the totalitarian states of the twentieth century; nevertheless a vigilant pressure to conformity was exerted by the Calvinist Church, and, on account of the continuing persecution of Catholics and Remonstrants, freedom of thought and religion had become the major issue of the day.

Hobbes was widely read in the Netherlands, and widely admired for a theory of government that was both comprehensive and secular, deriving its main principles from a study of human nature and without reference to the disputed evidence of revelation. At the same time, Hobbes provided no detailed theory of institutions, and the need for such a theory would not have escaped the readers of John Calvin's *Institutes*. Spinoza's *Theologico-Political Treatise* was an answer to both Hobbes and Calvin. Its first concern was to defend the principles of tolerance, moderation and self-limiting government. Like Hobbes, Spinoza derived his politics from a theory of human nature. But his exposition differs radically from that of his predecessor, involving a dual justification—religious and philosophical—for a single conception of the state. The two expositions correspond to the division between imagination and intellect. Since men are led by both forces, it is necessary to present arguments which appeal to both. Otherwise not every citizen will understand why he should accept the laws which govern him. Hence the emphasis, throughout the *Theologico-Political Treatise*, on biblical interpretation, Jewish law, and Christian apologetics: an emphasis to which I cannot here do justice, but which Spinoza himself regarded as of the first importance, not least because he thought (erroneously as it turned out) that it would exonerate him from the charge of irreligion.

Religion

True religion and true philosophy are identical, and consist in the intellectual love of God. All actual human religions, however, are based on a more passionate and temporal love. They see God *sub specie durationis*, and present him through the medium of inadequate and imaginative ideas. Often he is represented as possessing the finite passions of the human heart, and even the bodily form and countenance of humanity. However, 'the attributes which make man perfect can be as ill ascribed to God, as the attributes which make perfect the elephant and the ass can be assigned to man' (*C* XXIII). Men accustomed to worship an anthropomorphic God are more firmly rooted by their religious practice in the inadequate cognition which governs them. The best that can be hoped for them is that the strict examples from which they derive their spiritual nourishment should encapsulate, in however confused and metaphorical a form, the eternal truths of reason, and the intimations of a divine blessedness. Those parts of the scriptures which involve the enunciation of laws are therefore of the greatest weight, since these owe their authority, in the last instance, to an adequate idea of God. As for the stories and illustrations, Spinoza warns against the Christian habit of understanding 'oriental phrases' literally: the scriptures are of necessity written in 'the language of man', and Jewish readers are well versed in the habit of understanding such language allegorically:

> Scripture, when it says that God is angry with sinners, and that He is a Judge who takes cognizance of human actions, passes sentence on them, and judges them, is

93

speaking humanly, and in a way adapted to the received opinion of the masses; for its purpose is not to teach philosophy, nor to render men wise, but to make them obedient.
(*C* LXXVIII)

For men who live by imagination, this habit of obedience is the surest guide to peace and contentment. Religion is therefore a necessary ingredient in the life of the state, and its edicts and customs deserve the protection of the civil authorities.

Spinoza's distinction between the sublime conceptions of philosophy, and the superstitions of the multitude, is extremely important for an understanding of his politics. He recognizes man's dependence on beliefs which are irrational and even absurd; this dependence is both the foundation of social existence and the enduring obstacle to true political order. Spinoza rejects—as he must—all the major doctrines of anthropomorphic religion. Miracles are impossible, and the belief in them nothing more than a peculiarly exhilarating form of ignorance (*S* II, 24; *T* vi). The incarnation of God in Christ is also impossible—although the idea can be allegorically interpreted in ways which accord with a true idea of God (*C* LXXVIII). The conceptions of wrath, punishment, reward and compassion have no application to God, and it is a mistake to believe that God can be moved by our prayers or interested in fulfilling them.

At the same time, the worship of God is right and necessary, and 'in every church there are thoroughly honourable men, who worship God with justice and charity'. The distinctions between churches reflect modes of imagination, and there can be no philosophical reason— but at best only a political reason—for choosing between them. How then should the choice be made? Popular religion, which is the condition of peace among ignorant people, is also the cause of war between them. The state therefore has a duty to moderate between contending religious factions, and to ensure obedience only to that basic minimum of religious observance that would be acceptable to all reasonable men. Spinoza expressed his principle of toleration in broadly Christian language, so as to show his acceptance of the legally established religion. But 'as regards the Turks and other non-Christian nations: if they worship God by the practice of justice and charity towards their neighbour, I believe that they have the spirit of Christ and are in a state of salvation, whatever they may ignorantly hold regarding Mahomet and oracles' (*C* XLIII). Many passages make clear that Spinoza would have been prepared to countenance—in circumstances other than those which prevailed in the seventeenth-century Netherlands—a quite different institutional religion, provided it conformed to the requirement of toleration. The form of religion that should prevail is to be determined by the sovereign state, upon political grounds:

> Religion acquires its force as law solely from the decrees of the sovereign. God has no special kingdom among men except in so far as He reigns through temporal rulers. Moreover, the rites of religion and the outward observances of piety should be in accordance with the public peace and well-being, and should therefore be determined by the sovereign power. (*T* xix)

This subordination of religion to the temporal power applies only to the external observances, and has no bearing on the inner pathway to salvation. For the inner religion of the free man cannot be the subject of legislation:

inasmuch as [religion] consists not so much in outward actions as in simplicity and truth of character, it stands outside the law and public authority. Simplicity and truth of character are not produced by the constraint of laws, nor by the authority of the state . . .   (*T* vii)

Liberty

Since thought is governed by its own laws, and a man is compelled to conclusions not by the sovereign power but by the divine necessity of reason, there is something absurd in the attempt to control thought by legislation. Moreover, to curtail the expression of reason in public life is to destroy the greatest source of man's peace and harmony—the rational discussion of conflict, and the common pursuit of truth. Hence the real disturbers of the peace are those who, in a free state, seek to curtail the liberty of judgement over which they cannot tyrannize (*T* xx). No state can be in accordance with reason, therefore, without permitting freedom of thought and opinion:

the object of government is not to change men from rational beings into beasts or puppets, but to enable them to develop their minds and bodies in security, and to employ their reason unshackled; neither showing hatred, anger nor deceit, nor watched with the eyes of jealousy and injustice. In fact, the truc aim of government is liberty. (*T* xx)

Such freedom of thought and speech should not be confused with the freedom of action—and especially not with a freedom of action *through* speech. The calm utterance of what is sincerely thought to be true is a danger to no one; but the agitation of the mob through rhetoric— which fires the imagination while leaving the intellect untouched—is an inherent threat to lawful government. Moreover, freedom of conscience does not justify civil disobedience, but at best only dissent:

> supposing a man shows that a law is repugnant to sound reason, and should therefore be repealed; if he submits his opinion to the judgement of the supreme powers (who alone have the right of making and repealing laws), and meanwhile acts in no wise contrary to that law, he has deserved well of the state; but if he accuses the magistrates of iniquity, and stirs up the people against them, or if he seditiously strives to abrogate the law without their consent, he is a mere agitator (*perturbator*) and a rebel. (*T* xx)

This is because, in forming a state, citizens join in a social contract, and abrogate their right of free action to the sovereign body. But they do not, because they cannot, abrogate their right of free thought. The authorities therefore should concede free speech in so far as it is the necessary consequence of free thought, but not in so far as it involves action inconsistent with the legitimate demands of law and government.

Prophecy and politics

Spinoza's conception of the state is of a system of laws and institutions, organized so as to permit the influence of reason. He implicitly contrasts the power of philosophy, which is guided by reason, with that of faith, which is guided by prophecy. Men guided by prophecy attempt to order their affairs by appeal to ultimate revelations; such revelations may have no foundation in reason; nevertheless they are not to be questioned by the believer. Guided by wise prophets men may indeed be led peacefully to their betterment. But they may also be led astray.

97

The attempt to order our affairs by revelation leads to a peculiar kind of society—which we might call the 'prophetic order'. The prophetic order is at war with freedom of thought, and fiercely defensive of its sacred revelations; in such an order men are not united by free association under law, but led by the prophet towards a common goal, to which they must subscribe as the first condition of their allegiance. The prophetic order may survive without law, without civil institutions, and without liberal education and opinion. It faces the surrounding world with a mask of unyielding belligerence, feeling threatened in its very being by the rational thought whose voice it has vainly tried to silence.

The prophetic order is distinguished from the political order, in which the affairs of men are moderated and guided by reason, and in which therefore freedom of opinion is valued as the indispensable condition of government. The political order does not seek to unite men about a common purpose, but rather to permit the development of their multifarious purposes in such a way as to resolve the conflicts that arise between them. Its first principle of organization is therefore law, and it encourages the institutions whereby law develops in obedience to reason. These institutions are primarily secular, and the order of the state is a secular order, founded in compromise, tolerance and justice. The political order faces the surrounding world with a peaceful countenance, and seeks to settle differences with neighbours not through force, but through mutual agreement.

The contrast between the prophetic and the political orders motivates much of Spinoza's argument; it underlies his defence of limited government as much as his defence of civil and religious liberty, and leads him to advocate a kind of democracy as the best form of self-regulating politics. That such a modern system of political thought should have arisen from so medieval a metaphysics is not the least surprising result of Spinoza's philosophy.

Natural law and natural right

Grotius defended natural law as the foundation of sovereignty, and the final arbiter of human conflict. This law is implanted in us by reason, and God himself obeys it. If human beings do not obey the natural law it is because reason does not entirely govern their behaviour. The purpose of a legal system is to provide an effective substitute for reason in the motives of unreasonable men. Hobbes was not unsympathetic to such a defence of natural law. He added, however, that rights are nothing without the power which would enforce them, and therefore that power, not right, is the basic fact of politics.

Spinoza agreed in part with both philosophers, since he recognized no distinction between rights and powers, and no 'natural law' other than the one that the universe already obeys:

> as we are treating here of the universal power or right of nature we cannot here recognise any distinction between the desires engendered in us by reason, and those engendered by other causes, since the latter, as much as the former, are effects of nature, and display the *conatus* whereby a man endeavours to continue in existence. For man, be he learned or ignorant, is part of nature, and everything by which any man is determined to action, ought to be referred to the power of nature, i.e. to that power, as it is limited by the nature of this or that man. For man, whether guided by reason or mere desire, does nothing save in accordance with the laws and rules of nature, that is, by natural right (*ius naturae*). (*P* ii, 5)

It follows from this that he who has supreme power within a state also has the right to exercise that power. Like Grotius and Hobbes, Spinoza believed that this power is conferred upon the sovereign by a 'social contract', whereby men pass from the contending disorder of the 'state of nature' to the peace and cooperation of a civil society (*civitas*—see Glossary) (*T* xvi). For Spinoza such a contract effectively transfers the rights of the subject to his sovereign, except for those rights (or powers) which, because they belong to the essence of whatever possesses them, cannot be relinquished: 'no one can ever so utterly transfer to another his power and, consequently, his rights, as to cease to be a man' (*T* xvii). We can therefore reasonably be said to retain a 'natural right', in the more common sense of this expression, to all those things which constitute our inalienable powers: to life, limb and reason, and to such self-affirmation as is integral to the *conatus* which defines us. Hence 'the natural right of universal nature, and consequently of every individual thing, extends so far as its power' (*P* ii, 4): a doctrine which is distinctly favourable, incidentally, to the political pretensions of the philosopher.

Justice

It follows that man in a state of nature has little natural right. Only in society does he begin to have command over himself, and to perceive the true community of interests which unites him to his fellows, and enables him to augment his power by joining it to theirs. In a state of nature, guided by imagination, man perceives his fellows as inherently inimical, and strives weakly against them. In addition, lacking the power to impose justice on his neighbour, he lacks also the right to it; hence there is no wrongdoing (*peccatum*) in a state of nature. Only where there is sovereignty (*imperium*) is there justice and wrongdoing, both of which are therefore artefacts of man's political condition:

> Justice, therefore, and absolutely all the precepts of reason, including charity towards one's neighbour, receive the force of laws and ordinances only through the rights of sovereignty, that is . . . solely on the decree of those who possess the right to rule. (*T* xix)

Disobedience to the sovereign is therefore never justifiable on ground of justice, and the right of dominion is, in the end, self-legitimating. The subject owes his enhanced power to the civil society which protects him, and which confronts him at every point with the obligation to be ruled.

Although every sovereign body exercises a right to rule, not every political order is equally conducive to our happiness and liberty. Liberty therefore constitutes a criterion of perfection, whereby the various political orders may be distinguished one from another. The criterion is not to be understood in a consequentialist sense. Government is not simply to be seen as a means to liberty, since liberty is too intimately connected with political order to be regarded as a separable goal: it is, rather, the very *conatus* of the political organism, which cannot be detached from it, and which cannot be achieved except through the institutions of government.

'Constitutio libertatis'

The ideal political order is, in other words, a 'constitution of liberty', and a constitution (*iura*) is 'the soul of the sovereign body (*anima imperii*)' (*P* x, 9). Man needs political freedom in order to realize that other freedom which constitutes his happiness: 'a man is so far free, as he is led by reason; because so far is he determined to action by such causes as can be adequately understood by his unassisted nature' (*P* ii, 2). This 'causality of freedom' can rule over us only in a condition of free thought and communication. We are naturally prey to uncertainty and fear; our thoughts are liable to be dominated by the imagination, and we fall easy victim to the prophetic order which promises a passionate salvation. We may then welcome slavery as the end of fear and conflict, not realizing that 'peace is more than the mere absence of war, but rather a virtue which springs from the fortitude of the soul' (*P* v, 4); however, 'if slavery, barbarism and desolation are to be called peace, peace is the greatest misfortune that men can suffer' (*P* vi, 4). Such, in short, is Spinoza's answer to those who 'struggle for peace' in the name of a false prophetic order.

It is the political order alone which can establish the possibility of a genuine peace between people, and our allegiance to it is not a form of coercion or slavery, but on the contrary a form of freedom. In obeying the laws of a liberal constitution, we obey the dictates of reason, and to be compelled by reason is to be free. For the citizen of the liberal polity, therefore, civil disobedience, which threatens the condition upon which his freedom depends, involves only a partial understanding of what is at stake, and therefore an inadequate idea of his own motive. Such disobedience is an expression, not of freedom, but of inner bondage.

The first principle of political order is the free flow of opinion. Only if such a principle is satisfied can reason influence the conduct of politics without destroying the foundations of the state.

The nature of the state

A civil society is a form of corporate agency. While it has

individual human beings as its constituent parts, it also has a life and individuality of its own. In other words it has its own *conatus*, which confers on it the absolute right to preserve its own being. A civil society therefore 'does wrong when it does, or suffers to be done, things which may be the cause of its own ruin' (*P* iv, 4). The body politic, like the human body, may possess more or less power, more or less virtue, more or less freedom. Virtue, power and freedom are one and the same, and identical with reason. The task of politics is to build a constitution that is *obedient to reason*, just as the task of the individual person is to understand the laws of reason and submit to their sovereignty.

This submission of the state to reason is secured, not by the virtue of the ruler, but by the adoption of a constitution that makes the virtue of the ruler *irrelevant*: 'if a state is to be capable of lasting, its administration must be so organised that it does not matter whether its rulers are led by reason or passion' (*P* i, 6). In other words, the virtue of the state is achievable only by a constitution that limits the power of individuals, and ensures the independent reasonableness of the political process. Such a constitution could be monarchical, aristocratic or democratic. However, it is democracy (or at least, representative government unhampered by hereditary privilege) that is the best guarantee that power will be limited in the way that reason demands. More important than the procedure for acquiring and transferring power, however, is the internal division of power itself.

To vest the powers of state in one man or council is to reduce the independence of both the sovereign and the subject. The first, being the sole interpreter of the laws, lacks the motive to change them, while the second is constrained by a blind obedience. Hence 'contracts or laws, whereby the multitude transfers its right to a single council

103

or man, should without doubt be broken, when it is expedient for the general welfare to do so' (*P* iv, 6).

This does not mean that monarchy is necessarily an irrational form of government. For in a monarchy too power may be appropriately divided. Thus Spinoza (following Aristotle) advocates a privy council, formed according to a rule of rotation, whereby offices are successively filled by citizens who have demonstrated their fitness to hold them. It is also important to take away from those who exercise the sovereign power the sole right to interpret the law which sanctions their conduct. For 'those who administer or possess sovereignty always try to surround their high-handed actions with an aspect of legality (*specie iuris*), and to persuade the people that they act from good motives; this they are easily able to effect when they are the sole interpreters of the law' (*T* xvii). This 'appropriation' of the law by the executive arm of government can be prevented only if the judiciary is independent. Spinoza explains this idea through a biblical example:

> the power of evil-doing was greatly curtailed for the Hebrew captains by the fact that the whole interpretation of the law was vested in the Levites (Deut. xxi, 5) who, on their part, had no share in the government, and depended for all their support and consideration on a correct interpretation of the laws entrusted to them.
>
> (*T* ibid.)

Spinoza's argument for judicial independence constituted one of his most important political insights, and anticipated the constitutional theory—that of Montesquieu—which was to inspire the most thoroughly conceived 'constitution of liberty' that the modern world has known.

Some details

Spinoza's political recommendations are highly detailed, and not always derived with the rigour and clarity that a critic would require. Here, however, is a representative selection of them.

No lasting peace can be secured except by deterring political enemies. For this end, Spinoza argued, a citizen army is the most effective and rational device. Mercenary armies can conclude no lasting agreement on behalf of those they fight for, and will always prove disloyal to any agreement which they do not control. The history of the Netherlands proved that the towns could protect themselves only when the citizens were prepared to lay down their lives for their common salvation. In public as in private life (*E* 4, 58), therefore, honour may be required by reason, and is a part of power.

Power should be vested not in individuals but in the offices that they occupy. An office is at the same time a power conferred, and a power limited by its conferment. Only a rule of offices can lead to a power that is through and through responsive to the demands of reason, and detached from the passions of the man who exercises it.

This rule of offices was finely illustrated by the Dutch Estates General, which co-existed with the offices of Stadtholder and Grand Pensionary in mutual influence and mutual limitation. Spinoza believed that such a rule could be sustained only by ceremony and dignity. While reasonable men will see the intrinsic virtue of offices, the mass of mankind will always prefer the rule of prophets and figureheads, who claim a purely personal loyalty. Only ceremony can attract the imagination to look with favour on the offices whose true virtue it cannot understand.

The ruling principle of the offices of state must be secular and not religious. It is the state which has the final power to determine the rites of religion; and it is therefore the state that controls the formation and the dignity of office. Religion is an inner and not an outward condition, and can flourish in its true form only in that state 'where everyone's judgement is free and untrammelled, where each man may worship God as his conscience dictates, and where freedom is esteemed before all things clear and precious' (*T*, Preface). The prophetic order, which promises salvation, in fact destroys the conditions of our salvation, by sacrificing religion to its outward form, and so destroying the precious principle upon which peace and happiness depend: the respect for truth. It is not the prophetic order, but the political order, which has the final claim to be God's vicar on earth. Only in a secular state, therefore, can true religion flourish.

7 Spinoza's legacy

Spinoza's metaphysics contains a fatal flaw. Founded on the premise that reality corresponds to our adequate ideas, it proceeds without difficulty to the conclusion that we may have the same 'absolute' view of nature that we have of the universe of mathematics. Moreover, only if something is *causa sui* is the world really intelligible; otherwise our science, however comprehensive, explains the existence of nothing. But the premise is unwarranted, and the conclusions almost impossible to interpret. It seems that the world for Spinoza is *one* self-contained system, and that only one such system is possible. It seems also that the world is *two* self-contained systems, perhaps infinitely many. The distinction between substance and attribute is meant to remove the difficulty: however, the distinction is intelligible only on the supposition that there *is* no difficulty: that *one* thing can have two or more essences.

A century after Spinoza's death, Kant published his *Critique of Pure Reason*, arguing that no description of the world can free itself from the reference to human experience. Although the world that we know is not our creation, nor merely a synopsis of our perspective, it cannot be known except from the point of view that is ours. All attempts to break through the limits imposed by experience, and to know the world 'as it is in itself', from the absolute perspective of 'pure reason', end in contradiction—the kind of contradiction that we find in Spinoza's theory of the attributes. 'Ideas' of reason can never be coherently applied, and although we may have intimations of an absolute or 'transcendental' knowledge,

107

that knowledge can never be ours. These intimations are confined to moral life and aesthetic experience, and while they tell us, in a sense, what we really are, they can be translated into words only to speak unintelligibly.

The temptation of Pure Reason, Kant argued, can never be overcome. It is part of our nature as rational beings that we should seek to extend our reason indefinitely, so aspiring towards the 'transcendental' perspective which Spinoza called the 'aspect of eternity'. This yearning of reason towards the eternal is the source of all the speculative errors of metaphysics. But it is also the root of morality. Transformed into practical imperatives, the Ideas of Reason provide the moral law which guides us. The moral being, obedient to reason, may know in his actions what he vainly tries to utter in his words. Of all the great metaphysicians it was Spinoza who came nearest to saying how the world *would* be for us, were it possible to translate our moral knowledge into theories. Spinoza's thought is a projection into the infinite of the concrete sense of human dignity, and, in the distant clouds of metaphysics, its wonderful forms appear in sudden illumination, sharply outlined, and yet instantly vanishing as we reach for their meaning. If we find that meaning at last, it is only because we turn our eyes back towards ourselves, and recognize the truth of our dependence and our finitude.

Spinoza is right in believing that God's majesty is diminished by the idea that things might have been otherwise. The belief in miracles does no credit to God. For what need has God to intervene in events which he originates? The laws of the universe must be universally binding if we are to understand them: and it could not have been God's will to leave us forever ignorant of our situation. Spinoza is also right in his belief that truth is, in the end, our only yardstick, and that to live by any other standard is to be the victim of circumstance. There is implanted in every rational being the capacity to distinguish the true from the false, to weigh the evidence, and to confront the world without illusions. In this capacity our dignity resides, and in committing ourselves to truth we stand back from our immediate concerns and see the world as it should be seen—under the aspect of permanence. Truth cannot be fashionable, even if it so often offends. In the first shock of our encounter with truth, we may wish to turn away, to silence the person who utters it, to take refuge in that 'prophetic order' which promises a world according to our dreams, and sets us on the path to empty triumph. The political order, in which the shockingness of a world which makes no special place for us can be openly confessed to, is a rare achievement. Yet, if we are to sustain our dignity, we must work for such an order, in which all men can 'worship God in justice and charity'.

Our age is more dominated by scientific theory than was Spinoza's; but only a fond illusion persuades us that it is more guided by the truth. For we have seen superstition triumph on a scale that would have startled Spinoza, and which has been possible only because superstition has cloaked itself in the mantle of science. If the 'prophetic orders' of our day are the declared enemies of religion, this merely confirms, for the student of Spinoza, their superstitious character, and confirms, too, Spinoza's insight, that scientific objectivity and divine worship are the forms of intellectual freedom. Spinoza, like Pascal, saw that the new science must inevitably 'disenchant' the world. By following truth as our standard, we chase from their ancient abodes the miraculous, the sacred and the holy. The danger, however, is not that we follow this standard—for we have no other. It is that we follow it only so far as to lose our faith, and not so far as to gain it. We rid the world of useful superstitions, but continue to see it in fragmented form. Oppressed by its meaninglessness we succumb to new and less useful illusions—superstitions born of disenchantment, which are all the more dangerous for taking man, rather than God, as their object.

The remedy, Spinoza reminds us, is not to retreat into the pre-scientific worldview, but to go further along the path of disenchantment; losing both the old superstitions and the new, we discover at last a meaning in truth itself. By the very process which disenchants the world, we come to a new enchantment, recognizing God in everything, and loving his works in the very act of discovering them.

For Spinoza's intellectual contemporaries this 'religion of disenchantment' presented too great a challenge to be readily acceptable. Spinoza was accused of heresy and atheism. He occasionally tried to defend himself against such charges, asking 'whether a man throws off all religion, who maintains that God must be acknowledged as the highest good, and must, as such, be loved with a free mind?' (*C* XLIII). But what is this 'intellectual love of God', asked Leibniz, but 'trappings for the people'? 'There is nothing loveable', Leibniz added, 'in a God who does everything without choice and by necessity, without discrimination of good and evil.'

Spinoza's reputation survived the censorship with which his contemporaries sought to protect themselves from his arguments. But it was very soon eclipsed by the rise of the Leibnizian system in Germany, and the emergence in England of the empiricism of Locke, Berkeley and Hume. A biased entry in Bayle's *Dictionary*, published in 1697, provided the cultivated amateur with a convenient stereotype. Pierre Bayle was a learned French Huguenot who, living in exile in the Netherlands, came into contact with some of Spinoza's disciples. Although a fervent advocate of toleration, he denounced Spinoza as a 'systematic atheist', and provided a sketch of the philosopher's life and opinions which was for a long time regarded as definitive, being later reproduced by the authors of the *Encyclopédie*. Spinoza's star declined, and rose again only in the glorious twilight of romanticism. For the poet Novalis, and the theologian Schleiermacher, Spinoza suddenly lost his character of cynic and atheist, becoming instead the model of the religious believer, the god-intoxicated philosopher, in whose system the archetype of faith is directly encountered.

Two contemporaries of Kant—Jacobi and Moses Mendelssohn—had corresponded about Spinoza's system, and Jacobi published his letters in the form of a book. The level of discussion that followed upon this performance would hardly have gladdened Spinoza, consisting as it did largely of romantic and mystical speculations on the theme of the oneness of the world and the immanence of God. Herder, however, was more discriminating, spending long hours in the study of Spinoza, and writing of the profound impression made upon him by the thought that whosoever loves God, cannot endeavour to bring it about that God should love him in return (*E* 5, 19). The same stunning proposition is mentioned by Goethe, in a beautiful page of his autobiography. But the solemn abstraction is transformed into a breathless, palpitating record of a poetic moment:

That wonderful utterance: 'whosoever loves God, cannot strive that God should love him in return', with all the preceding sentences upon which it rests, with all the following sentences which spring from it, filled my entire meditation. To be in everything unselfish, to the highest unselfishness in love and friendship, was my

111

greatest desire, my maxim, my rule, and so that insolent remark which follows—'if I love you, what is that to you?'—was for me spoken directly into my heart.

Goethe adds that Spinoza's calm and abstract style sorted so ill with his own unruly passions, that he was a most unhappy student of the pages which offered to justify this powerful utterance. Nevertheless it was Goethe who performed the greatest service on Spinoza's behalf, denouncing the article in Bayle's *Dictionary*, and upholding, as the first of Spinoza's achievements, the attack on superstition in the name of God.

Spinoza the philosopher emerged in his true colours through the work of Schelling and Hegel. In Hegel's system, indeed, the major arguments of the *Ethics* are appropriated and transformed. The theory of the one substance becomes that of the Absolute Idea—the single entity which is realized in and through the attributes of nature, spirit, art and history. The theory of adequate ideas becomes the dialectic, according to which knowledge is a progressive advance from a confused and 'abstract' 'positing' of a concept, to the ever completer, ever more 'absolute' conception of the world. The theory of *conatus* becomes that of 'self-realization' through the successive 'objectifications' of the spirit; the theory of political order becomes that of the state as the realization of freedom, and the 'march of reason in the world'. The sublime impertinence of Hegel is to have combined these Spinozist conceptions with the idea which they deny— the idea of the self, as the historically determined, limited and partial viewpoint upon the world, whose process of self-realization is also the actuality and the meaning of all that there is. Hegel summed up the transformation in characteristic terms, ostentatiously displaying his own achievement by refraining from naming himself as the author of it:

> As against Spinoza, again, it is to be noted that the mind in the judgement by which it 'constitutes' itself an 'ego' (a free subject . . .) has emerged from substance, and that the philosophy which gives this judgement as the absolute characteristic of mind has emerged from Spinozism. (*Encyc*. section 415)

Hegel's philosophy was the crowning moment of German romanticism, and also the self-conscious announcement of its end. By a curious accident, the Marxian inversion of Hegel (the 'setting of Hegel upon his feet') proved equally favourable to Spinoza, whose dictum that 'the mind is the idea of the body' was at once compared to the dictum of Marx and Engels, that 'life determines consciousness, not consciousness life' (*The German Ideology*). The Marxists began to find in Spinoza's theory of mind a premonition of the 'dialectical materialism' which they saw in Marx, and to interpret Spinoza's epistemology as a proto-Marxian theory of ideology.

Spinoza would have recoiled from Marxism, with its false claim to science, its superstitious belief in a transformed human nature, and its advocacy of a new prophetic order in which man will live free from the institutions of compromise and law. Nevertheless, it is, as the Marxists say, 'no accident' that his philosophy should have found such a direct parallel in the thinking of a prophetic atheist, for whom man's endeavours are inseparable from his material circumstances, and governed by comprehensive natural laws. It is likewise no accident that Spinoza should have called forth so sharp an attack from the other false prophet of atheism, Nietzsche, who hated the Spinozist view that the truth is separable from our perspective upon it:

[Philosophers] all pose as though their real opinions had been discovered and attained through the self-evolving of a cold, pure, divinely indifferent dialectic . . . whereas, in fact, a prejudiced proposition, idea or 'suggestion', which is generally their heart's desire abstracted and refined, is defended by them with arguments sought out after the event . . . [thus] the hocus-pocus in mathematical form, by means of which Spinoza has as it were clad his philosophy in mail and mask—in fact, the 'love of *his* wisdom', to translate the term fairly and squarely—in order thereby to strike terror at once into the heart of the assailant who should dare to cast a glance on that invincible maiden, that Pallas Athene:—how much of personal timidity and vulnerability does this mask of a sickly recluse betray!

(*Beyond Good and Evil* 1, 5)

Whatever the weaknesses of Spinoza's system, one is tempted to think that a philosopher cannot be wholly wrong, who calls forth such a quantity of spite in someone who would have agreed, had he understood his argument, with so much of what he said.

Glossary

This glossary is offered as a guide to principal terms, many of which are translated in conflicting ways in the available English language editions.

affectio: emotion, i.e. an 'affection' of a human being which is also a *passio* (q.v.).

affectus: an 'affect', i.e. a condition of a thing which is brought about by external circumstances. Hence (when referring to mental items) an emotion. There is considerable uncertainty as to whether Spinoza used '*affectio*' and '*affectus*' as synonyms.

amor intellectualis Dei: the intellectual love of God.

attributum: attribute (a technical term, defined in *E* 1, Definition 4, whose use is to be distinguished from the usual sense of 'attribute' in Aristotelian logic).

causa sui: cause of itself (defined contentiously in *E* 1, Definition 1).

civitas: civil society, i.e. a society organized within, but distinct from, a *respublica* (q.v.).

cognitio: cognition (rendered by some translators as 'knowledge', a practice which leads to such odd locutions as 'false knowledge').

conatus: not translated (some translators use the words 'endeavour' or 'striving').

corpus: material object — literally 'body'.

formaliter: 'formally', i.e. pertaining to the real essence of something (see *objective*).

idea: idea. Covers the modern uses of 'concept', 'proposition', 'thought', but also includes any other concept of a mental item.

ideatum: not translated — the extended item which 'corresponds' to a given idea. Some translators use the word 'object', others the word 'ideal'. Both are misleading (see *objective*).

imperium: sovereignty. Some translators give 'dominion' or 'power'.

modus: mode, a technical term defined in *E* 1, Definition 5.

motus et quies: motion and rest — the infinite mode which is expressed in the laws of physics.

objective: 'objectively', i.e. pertaining to the representation of something in the mind, as opposed to *formaliter*, pertaining to its essential reality.

objectum: the object (of an idea, emotion etc.), i.e. that which is represented in the mind, as opposed to the *ideatum*, that which corresponds to the idea in material reality.

passio: passion, i.e. a state of the mind or body in relation to which we are 'passive'.

quatenus: in so far as. A technical term, used to represent impassable barriers as passable. (See Chapter 4, section 4.)

respublica: state, i.e. an organized system of *imperium*. (The distinction between *civitas* and *respublica* prefigures that made by Hegel between civil society and state—hence my translation.)

scientia intuitiva: intuition. (A mental act in which a valid proof is immediately grasped and accepted as true.)

substantia: substance, a prime technical term defined in *E* 1, Definition 3.

sub specie aeternitatis: under the aspect of eternity.

sub specie durationis: under the aspect of time (or of duration).

For further information on Spinoza's terminology, see the Glossary-Index to E. Curley's edition of Spinoza's works (cited opposite), and E. Giancotti Boscherini, *Lexicon Spinozanum* (The Hague, 1970).

Further reading

Writings by Spinoza
The works of Spinoza exist in several English versions. The most readily available of these is that by R. H. M. Elwes (revised edition, London, 1903, reprinted in 1955 by Dover Publications). This contains the *Ethics*, the three treatises, and a selection of the correspondence. The translation is unsystematic and very misleading. More systematic but often equally misleading is the Everyman edition of the *Ethics* and the *Treatise on the Emendation of the Intellect*, (tr. Andrew Boyle, London, 1910, reprinted in 1977).

A complete and informative edition of the *Correspondence* has been prepared by A. Wolf (London, 1928, reissued in 1966). This is perhaps the best introduction to Spinoza's philosophy. In referring to Spinoza's letters I use the numbering given by Wolf. The same editor has prepared a scholarly edition of the *Short Treatise on God, Man and His Well-Being* (London, 1910). References in the text are to this edition, which also contains an agreeable biography of Spinoza.

The *Principles of Cartesian Philosophy* and the *Metaphysical Thoughts* are available in one volume from Open Court publishers (tr. Halbert Hains Britan, 1905, reprinted 1974).

A scholarly edition of a part of the *Tractatus Theologico-Politicus* and the surviving parts of the *Tractatus Politicus* is available, edited by A. G. Wernham, under the title of *Spinoza, The Political Works*, Oxford, 1958. This contains a useful introduction, and prints the Latin text alongside the English translation.

There is also now available an expensive but impressively edited volume containing the *Ethics*, the *Treatise on the Emendation of the Intellect*, the *Short Treatise on God, Man and His Well-Being*, *Descartes' Principles of Philosophy and Metaphysical Thoughts* and Spinoza's letters from the periods when these works were composed. This is edited and translated by Edwin Curley (Princeton, 1985). A second volume will contain the remaining letters and political works. It is to be expected that Curley's edition will provide the definitive text for English readers.

117

Spinoza

Writings about Spinoza

The early biographies of Spinoza—by Colerus and Meyer—make interesting reading. Perhaps the best biography in English is that contained in Sir Frederick Pollock's *Spinoza: His Life and Philosophy* (London, 1880, second edition 1912).

Among older commentaries, that by John Caird (Edinburgh and London, 1888) is in many ways the most instructive, in showing just what Spinoza meant to a philosopher who accepted a large part of his metaphysics. Also useful—though very dated—is the treatise on *The Philosophy of Spinoza* by Harry Austyn Wolfson (Cambridge, Mass., 2 vols., 1934, reprinted in one volume 1983).

An abridged version of the article on Spinoza from Bayle's *Dictionary* can be found in E. A. Beller and M. du P. Lee Jr (eds.), *Selections from Bayle's Dictionary* (Princeton, 1952).

Among more modern commentaries, that by Sir Stuart Hampshire (Penguin Books, 1951, reprinted 1981), remains the most succinct and rewarding, although a recent work by Jonathan Bennett (*A Study of Spinoza's Ethics*, Cambridge, 1984) provides a useful application of the analytical method to Spinoza's arguments.

Several useful collections of essays exist, the best being S. Paul Kashap's *Studies in Spinoza: Critical and Interpretive Essays* (Berkeley, 1972), Marjorie Grene's *Spinoza, a Collection of Critical Essays* (Notre Dame, Indiana, 1973), and Robert W. Shahan and J. Biro's *Spinoza: New Perspectives* (Norman, Oklahoma, 1978).

The work of Thomas Carson Mark referred to in Chapter 4 is 'The Spinozistic Attributes', *Philosophia* 7 (1977). The same author's *Spinoza's Theory of Truth* (Columbia University Press, 1972) is a useful contribution on the most difficult aspects of Spinoza's epistemology, a topic also treated in G. H. R. Parkinson's *Spinoza's Theory of Knowledge* (Oxford, Clarendon Press, 1954, reprinted 1964).

On the political philosophy the most accessible commentary is that of Robert J. McShea (*The Political Philosophy of Spinoza*, New York & London, 1968).

Index

OXFORD

MORE OXFORD PAPERBACKS

This book is just one of nearly 1000 Oxford Paper-
backs currently in print. If you would like details of
other Oxford Paperbacks, including titles in the
World's Classics, Oxford Reference, Oxford
Books, OPUS, Past Masters, Oxford Authors, and
Oxford Shakespeare series, please write to:

UK and Europe: Oxford Paperbacks Publicity Man-
ager, Arts and Reference Publicity Department,
Oxford University Press, Walton Street, Oxford
OX2 6DP.

Customers in UK and Europe will find Oxford
Paperbacks available in all good bookshops. But in
case of difficulty please send orders to the Cash-
with-Order Department, Oxford University Press
Distribution Services, Saxon Way West, Corby,
Northants NN18 9ES. Tel: 01536 741519; Fax:
01536 746337. Please send a cheque for the total cost
of the books, plus £1.75 postage and packing for
orders under £20; £2.75 for orders over £20. Customers outside the UK should add 10% of the cost
of the books for postage and packing.

USA: Oxford Paperbacks Marketing Manager,
Oxford University Press, Inc., 200 Madison Av-
enue, New York, N.Y. 10016.

Canada: Trade Department, Oxford University
Press, 70 Wynford Drive, Don Mills, Ontario M3C
1J9.

Australia: Trade Marketing Manager, Oxford University Press, G.P.O. Box 2784Y, Melbourne 3001,
Victoria.

South Africa: Oxford University Press, P.O. Box
1141, Cape Town 8000.

PAST MASTERS

A wide range of unique, short, clear introductions to the lives and work of the world's most influential thinkers. Written by experts, they cover the history of ideas from Aristotle to Wittgenstein. Readers need no previous knowledge of the subject, so they are ideal for students and general readers alike.

Each book takes as its main focus the thought and work of its subject. There is a short section on the life and a final chapter on the legacy and influence of the thinker. A section of further reading helps in further research.

The series continues to grow, and future Past Masters will include **Owen Gingerich** on *Copernicus*, **R G Frey** on *Joseph Butler*, **Bhiku Parekh** on *Gandhi*, **Christopher Taylor** on *Socrates*, **Michael Inwood** on *Heidegger*, and **Peter Ghosh** on *Weber*.

MASTERS

KEYNES

Robert Skidelsky

John Maynard Keynes is a central thinker of the twentieth century. This is the only available short introduction to his life and work.

Keynes's doctrines continue to inspire strong feelings in admirers and detractors alike. This short, engaging study of his life and thought explores the many positive and negative stereotypes and also examines the quality of Keynes's mind, his cultural and social milieu, his ethical and practical philosophy, and his monetary thought. Recent scholarship has significantly altered the treatment and assessment of Keynes's contribution to twentieth-century economic thinking, and the current state of the debate initiated by the Keynesian revolution is discussed in a final chapter on its legacy.

MASTERS

RUSSELL

A. C. Grayling

Bertrand Russell (1872–1970) is one of the most famous and important philosophers of the twentieth century. In this account of his life and work A. C. Grayling introduces both his technical contributions to logic and philosophy, and his wide-ranging views on education, politics, war, and sexual morality. Russell is credited with being one of the prime movers of Analytic Philosophy, and with having played a part in the revolution in social attitudes witnessed throughout the twentieth-century world. This introduction gives a clear survey of Russell's achievements across their whole range.

PHILOSOPHY IN OXFORD PAPERBACKS
THE GREAT PHILOSOPHERS
Bryan Magee

Beginning with the death of Socrates in 399, and following the story through the centuries to recent figures such as Bertrand Russell and Wittgenstein, Bryan Magee and fifteen contemporary writers and philosophers provide an accessible and exciting introduction to Western philosophy and its greatest thinkers.

Bryan Magee in conversation with:

A. J. Ayer	John Passmore
Michael Ayers	Anthony Quinton
Miles Burnyeat	John Searle
Frederick Copleston	Peter Singer
Hubert Dreyfus	J. P. Stern
Anthony Kenny	Geoffrey Warnock
Sidney Morgenbesser	Bernard Williams
Martha Nussbaum	

'Magee is to be congratulated . . . anyone who sees the programmes or reads the book will be left in no danger of believing philosophical thinking is unpractical and uninteresting.' Ronald Hayman, *Times Educational Supplement*

'one of the liveliest, fast-paced introductions to philosophy, ancient and modern that one could wish for' *Universe*

OPUS

General Editors: Walter Bodmer,
Christopher Butler, Robert Evans,
John Skorupski

CLASSICAL THOUGHT

Terence Irwin

Spanning over a thousand years from Homer to Saint Augustine, *Classical Thought* encompasses a vast range of material, in succinct style, while remaining clear and lucid even to those with no philosophical or Classical background.

The major philosophers and philosophical schools are examined—the Presocratics, Socrates, Plato, Aristotle, Stoicism, Epicureanism, Neoplatonism; but other important thinkers, such as Greek tragedians, historians, medical writers, and early Christian writers, are also discussed. The emphasis is naturally on questions of philosophical interest (although the literary and historical background to Classical philosophy is not ignored), and again the scope is broad—ethics, the theory of knowledge, philosophy of mind, philosophical theology. All this is presented in a fully integrated, highly readable text which covers many of the most important areas of ancient thought and in which stress is laid on the variety and continuity of philosophical thinking after Aristotle.

THE OXFORD AUTHORS

General Editor: Frank Kermode

THE OXFORD AUTHORS is a series of authoritative editions of major English writers. Aimed at both students and general readers, each volume contains a generous selection of the best writings—poetry, prose, and letters—to give the essence of a writer's work and thinking. All the texts are complemented by essential notes, an introduction, chronology, and suggestions for further reading.

Matthew Arnold
William Blake
Lord Byron
John Clare
Samuel Taylor Coleridge
John Donne
John Dryden
Ralph Waldo Emerson
Thomas Hardy
George Herbert and Henry Vaughan
Gerard Manley Hopkins
Samuel Johnson
Ben Jonson
John Keats
Andrew Marvell
John Milton
Alexander Pope
Sir Philip Sidney
Oscar Wilde
William Wordsworth

THE OXFORD AUTHORS
BEN JONSON
Edited by Ian Donaldson

Ben Jonson's literary reputation with his contemporaries rivalled, and perhaps surpassed, that of Shakespeare. This edition presents the full texts of Jonson's two most popular comedies, *Volpone* and *The Alchemist* and of his commonplace book *Discoveries*, his *Conversations with William Drummond of Hawthornden*, and all his non-dramatic poetry. To this is added a generous selection of songs and poems from the plays and masques, and a number of poems doubtfully attributed to Jonson.

THE OXFORD AUTHORS

SIR PHILIP SIDNEY

Edited by Katherine Duncan-Jones

Born in 1554, Sir Philip Sidney was hailed as the perfect Renaissance patron, soldier, lover, and courtier, but it was only after his untimely death at the age of thirty-two that his literary achievements were truly recognized.

This collection ranges more widely through Sidney's works than any previous volume and includes substantial parts of both versions of the *Arcadia*, *A Defence of Poesy*, and the whole of the sonnet sequence *Astrophil and Stella*. Supplementary texts, such as his letters and the numerous elegies which appeared after his death, help to illustrate the wide spectrum of his achievements, and the admiration he inspired in his contemporaries.

Oxford
Paperback
Reference

OXFORD PAPERBACK REFERENCE

From *Art and Artists* to *Zoology*, the Oxford Paperback Reference series offers the very best subject reference books at the most affordable prices.

Authoritative, accessible, and up to date, the series features dictionaries in key student areas, as well as a range of fascinating books for a general readership. Included are such well-established titles as Fowler's *Modern English Usage*, Margaret Drabble's *Concise Companion to English Literature*, and the bestselling science and medical dictionaries.

The series has now been relaunched in handsome new covers. Highlights include new editions of some of the most popular titles, as well as brand new paperback reference books on *Politics*, *Philosophy*, and *Twentieth-Century Poetry*.

With new titles being constantly added, and existing titles regularly updated, Oxford Paperback Reference is unrivalled in its breadth of coverage and expansive publishing programme. New dictionaries of *Film*, *Economics*, *Linguistics*, *Architecture*, *Archaeology*, *Astronomy*, and *The Bible* are just a few of those coming in the future.

**Oxford
Paperback
Reference**

THE CONCISE OXFORD COMPANION
TO ENGLISH LITERATURE

*Edited by Margaret Drabble and
Jenny Stringer*

Derived from the acclaimed *Oxford Companion to
English Literature*, the concise maintains the wide
coverage of its parent volume. It is an indispensable,
compact guide to all aspects of English literature.
For this revised edition, existing entries have been
fully updated and revised with 60 new entries added
on contemporary writers.

* **Over 5,000 entries on the lives and works of
  authors, poets and playwrights**

* **The most comprehensive and authoritative
  paperback guide to English literature**

* **New entries include Peter Ackroyd, Martin
  Amis, Toni Morrison, and Jeanette Winterson**

* **New appendices list major literary prize-
  winners**

From the reviews of its parent volume:

'It earns its place at the head of the best sellers: every
home should have one'
Sunday Times

Oxford
Paperback
Reference

THE CONCISE OXFORD DICTIONARY
OF MUSIC

New Edition

Edited by Michael Kennedy

Derived from the full *Oxford Dictionary of Music* this is the most authoritative and up-to-date dictionary of music available in paperback. Fully revised and updated for this new edition, it is a rich mine of information for lovers of music of all periods and styles.

* **14,000 entries on musical terms, works, composers, librettists, musicians, singers and orchestras.**

* **Comprehensive work-lists for major composers**

* **Generous coverage of living composers and performers**

'clearly the best around . . . the dictionary that everyone should have'
Literary Review

'indispensable'
Yorkshire Post

THE CONCISE OXFORD DICTIONARY
OF OPERA

New Edition

Edited by Ewan West and John Warrack

Derived from the full *Oxford Dictionary of Opera*, this is the most authoritative and up-to-date dictionary of opera available in paperback. Fully revised for this new edition, it is designed to be accessible to all those who enjoy opera, whether at the opera-house or at home.

* Over 3,500 entries on operas, composers, and performers

* Plot summaries and separate entries for well-known roles, arias, and choruses

* Leading conductors, producers and designers

From the reviews of its parent volume:

'the most authoritative single-volume work of its kind'
Independent on Sunday

'an invaluable reference work'
Gramophone

OPUS

A HISTORICAL INTRODUCTION TO THE PHILOSOPHY OF SCIENCE

John Losee

This challenging introduction, designed for readers without an extensive knowledge of formal logic or of the history of science, looks at the long-argued questions raised by philosophers and scientists about the proper evaluation of scientific interpretations. It offers an historical exposition of differing views on issues such as the merits of competing theories; the interdependence of observation and theory; and the nature of scientific progress. The author looks at explanations given by Plato, Aristotle, and Pythagoras, and through to Bacon and Descartes, to Nagel, Kuhn, and Laudan.

This edition incorporates an extended discussion of contemporary developments and changes within the history of science, and examines recent controversies and the search for a non-prescriptive philosophy of science.

'a challenging interdisciplinary work'
New Scientist